CRANE BROTHERS' ROUTE
'RUNNING THE HIMALAYAS'

More than 2000 miles and 280,000 feet of climbing over 65 mountain passes

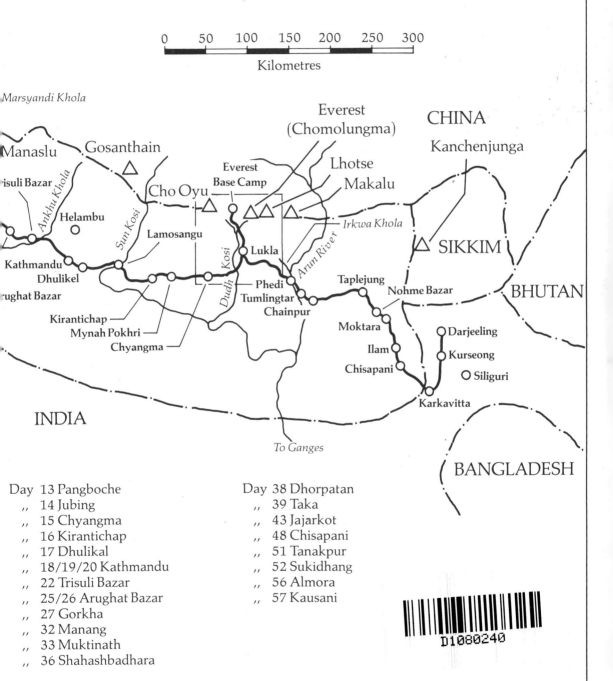

```
0    50   100   150   200   250   300
```
Kilometres

Marsyandi Khola

Manaslu   Gosanthain   Everest (Chomolungma)   CHINA

Kanchenjunga

isuli Bazar   *Ankhu Khola*   Everest Base Camp   Lhotse   Makalu

Cho Oyu

Helambu   *Sun Kosi*   Lamosangu

Irkwa Khola

SIKKIM   BHUTAN

Lukla

Kathmandu
Dhulikel
rughat Bazar

Dudh Kosi

Arun River

Phedi   Taplejung
Tumlingtar   Nohme Bazar
Chainpur

Kirantichap
Mynah Pokhri
Chyangma

Moktara

Darjeeling
Kurseong

Ilam

Siliguri

Chisapani

Karkavitta

INDIA

To Ganges

BANGLADESH

Day 13 Pangboche
 ,, 14 Jubing
 ,, 15 Chyangma
 ,, 16 Kirantichap
 ,, 17 Dhulikal
 ,, 18/19/20 Kathmandu
 ,, 22 Trisuli Bazar
 ,, 25/26 Arughat Bazar
 ,, 27 Gorkha
 ,, 32 Manang
 ,, 33 Muktinath
 ,, 36 Shahashbadhara

Day 38 Dhorpatan
 ,, 39 Taka
 ,, 43 Jajarkot
 ,, 48 Chisapani
 ,, 51 Tanakpur
 ,, 52 Sukidhang
 ,, 56 Almora
 ,, 57 Kausani

D1080240

RUNNING THE HIMALAYAS

RUNNING THE HIMALAYAS

Richard and Adrian Crane

Foreword by Lord Hunt of Llanfair Waterdine, KG, KT, CBE, DSO

NEW ENGLISH LIBRARY

First published in Great Britain in 1984 by
New English Library, Mill Road, Dunton Green,
Sevenoaks, Kent. Editorial office:
47 Bedford Square, London WC1B 3DP.

Typeset by Rowland Phototypesetting Ltd, Bury St Edmunds, Suffolk.
Printed in Great Britain by Hazell, Watson and Viney Ltd,
Member of the BPCC Group, Aylesbury, Bucks, and
bound by Dorstel Press, Harlow.

British Library Cataloguing in Publication Data

Crane, Richard
   Running the Himalayas.
   1. Running – Himalaya Mountains
   2. Himalaya Mountains – Description and travel
   I. Title   II. Crane, Adrian
   915.4'0452   DS485.H6

   ISBN 0-450-06082-9

To Mum

It is thanks to the following sponsors that 'Running the Himalayas' was taken from an idea to a success.

Air India	Baggage transportation
Al-Trak Engineering Ltd	Help and advice on overland transport
Associated Biscuits Ltd	Travel expenses and 'goodies'
Banon's Hotel, Manali, India	Accommodation and local advice
Barrod Bennett	Map expenses
Blacks Ltd/Alpine Sports	Mountaineering equipment
British Home Stores	Thermal underwear, socks
British Petroleum	Opportunity
Charles Crane	Office facilities
Cobra Sports Shoe Shops	Contribution to expenses
Don Young	Contribution to expenses
Explor-Asia	Communication and travel services
Flashmans Hotel, Rawalpindi	Finishing reception
Gore, W.L. & Associates	Gore-Tex weather suits
Government of Pakistan	Hospitality
Himalayan Mountaineering Institute	Accommodation and advice
Indian Mountaineering Foundation	Advice
Indian Airlines	Logistic and communication help
Karrimor International Ltd	Rucksacks, duvets, sleeping bags
Lunn Poly	Travel services
Malla Hotel, Kathmandu	Accommodation
May and Baker	Medical supplies
Metal Box P.L.C.	Contribution to expenses
Molly and Betty	Paper-pushing
Mountain Travel/Tiger Tops Nepal	Logistic, communication service and local advice
New Balance Ltd	Running shoes, expenses
Nigel Geary and John Klon	Water carrier
Project Resources Inc.	Opportunity
Scholl U.K. Ltd	Footcare products, expenses
Systems Informatics/S.I.F.O.	Contribution to expenses
Townend, Dr	Medical services and advice
Troll Ltd	Gore-Tex weather suits
Wellcome Foundation Ltd	Medical supplies
West London Institute	Fitness testing
Whitworths Ltd	Dried fruit
Wilkinson Sword Ltd	Disposable lighters

Acknowledgements

Our adventure in the Himalayas could not have happened without the warmth and love of our family behind us. We owe many happy childhood days to our brother Chris and sisters Bar, Jo, Sarah and Emmy. We learnt our mountain skills from our Dad and our Uncle Hol and his merry band of winter climbers. We acquired what social skills we have from the lads and lasses of Keswick School, the students at Durham University and assorted riffraff around the world.

We believe that we would not have progressed far with this grisly expedition if we had not been raising funds for the charity Intermediate Technology. We knew that every step we took was one step closer to ending poverty in this world.

Richard and Adrian Crane

Contents

Foreword

by Lord Hunt of Llanfair Waterdine, KG, KT, CBE, DSO

This is the story of an astonishing feat of enterprise and endurance by two very remarkable young men. I have only the vaguest inkling of what they endured in the course of their journey along the whole range of the highest mountains in the world – all 2000 miles of it – within 101 days. A small personal sample of the odds they faced may serve to indicate my sense of the dimension of their achievement, from my own experience of many years of Himalayan travel. Forty-four years ago, my wife and I made a 'forced march' from a base camp beneath Kangchenjunga to Darjeeling, a distance of 70 miles, in 48 hours, in response to an urgent order to myself to report for active service in Europe at the beginning of the last war. We arrived in an advanced state of exhaustion after travelling 35 miles a day over a small section of the kind of terrain covered by Richard and Adrian Crane. Any thought of continuing our journey for one more day, let alone for another 99 days, would have been unimaginably awful.

As one who now prefers a more leisurely enjoyment of those great mountains: their stupendous scenery, their lovable peoples and – even for the elderly – their challenges, I salute the brothers Crane for their tenacity and courage. I commend their story, not only for its graphic, earthy descriptions of what it felt like in human suffering, but also for its perception, despite the aches and pains, of those wonderful mountains and of the folk who live among them. I commend all the more because the purpose of their performance was, in part, to east the burden of the handicaps which go with life in the highlands of the Himalaya.

31.5.1984

PROLOGUE

On the Road to Failure

'WE'RE BEATEN. We can't go any further.' The light was weak and I could hardly see to write in my diary. 'We're properly exhausted now. We set out to run the Himalayas and we can't even run to Kathmandu. What a couple of failures we are!' I dropped my pencil, closed my diary and lowered my weary body down to the ground beside my brother Adrian.

Three ragged and rascally-looking locals edged their curiosity a shade closer. A Nepalese dog howled in the distance, mosquitoes buzzed around my eyes and something, probably ants, crawled up my shorts, but I only remember thinking 'sod the lot' before sleep hit me like a sledgehammer.

I woke at five, at the first cruel light of dawn. The whole of me was leaden, heavy, moulded into the earth. If I were simply to close my eyes again, I need never get up. I could dream.

Slowly I levered myself up on my elbows and focused on reality. We had set out to do something never tackled before: to race across some of the toughest terrain in the world. Up mountain paths, over glaciers, through thin air and down along dusty trails – possibly 2500 miles from Darjeeling in India to Rawalpindi in Pakistan. The length of the Himalayas.

Now, here we were: we'd covered more than 400 miles in seventeen days, picked our way through thirty mountain passes, some days climbing 12,000 feet, and we were stuck a mere marathon's worth of miles from Kathmandu.

Bloody hell! We could crawl there in a day. If we could crawl.

I looked at Adrian. He was still sound asleep. Flat on his back, his limp limbs splayed as though he'd been thrown backwards from fifty feet. His head was twisted back and his mouth was wide open. You could see he hadn't used a toothbrush for days. His lips were cracked; his nose, sunburnt, was raw-red and peeling. His jaw was covered with tufty bits of beard. Altogether a nasty sight.

I guess I was also pretty smelly. The cotton shirts and shorts we wore were filthy. We hadn't taken them off since we started, and seventeen days of sweat and grime had starched them stiff. Salt stains marked the outline of our rucksacks, and our sleeves and shirt tails were smeared from wiping our hands and noses. We were past caring. In fact, we'd abandoned any thought of tidiness when we first planned the expedition because razors and combs and soap would add to the weight we had to carry. But carry on we had to.

1

I reached across and shook my brother. Shook him gently, but it was enough to start a violent judder in his breathing before his snoring stalled altogether. For a long moment he lay there with hardly a twitch, then his mouth closed and you could see his waking struggle to surface from somewhere deep way down.

It must have been painful, for he moaned and muttered a few incomprehensible words which obviously meant 'Give us a break.'

'C'mon, Ados,' I said, my firmness accentuated by his nickname. 'We've got to get going.'

I was also trying to convince myself. It was all very well lying there determined to press on, but actually getting up was another matter. With an effort I hauled myself to my feet, stretched my aches cautiously and bent to the task of rolling up my sleeping bag, stuffing it into my rucksack.

I was afraid to ask Ados how he felt in case he might be encouraged to persuade me that he was too ill to carry on. As it was, I knew he'd been running on gut rot through unaccustomed heat to exhaustion, and if I gave him the opportunity he might opt for surrender. It's not that he give up easily, not at all, but Ados has a capacity for being philosophical about failure. He can shrug it off. I'm more neurotic about it and the humiliation that can accompany it. But it wasn't fear that compelled me then. Having, more or less, breezed through the run up from Darjeeling to the 18,000 feet of Everest Base Camp, we'd kicked off from there determined to beat the old mail-runners time for the 164 miles to Kathmandu.

One optimistic calculation had us believing it could be done in three days, but the trail doesn't run downhill all the way. On the contrary, you're running 'across the grain' of Nepal – ridge after ridge rear like mountainous waves in front of you. No sooner are you over the top of one pass and down the other side, than you're climbing again. Thirteen mountain passes with 32,000 feet of climbing to be exact.

Now we were only a hobbling distance from a five-and-a-half-day time for this particular section. Compared with the usual trek of two to three weeks, it would be an achievement worth taking home with us. A good consolation prize.

I knew that as long as I was leading, Ados would follow. Alone, he might say 'What the hell' and lie down again, but not if I was busting to get someplace.

Rather gingerly he pulled himself together and packed his pains for another effort. Without a word he followed me, shuffling down the trail. We took it very slowly, walking to ease the stiffness that had seized us. But after a few hundred yards, Adrian's diarrhoea caught up with him. Hardly bothering to move off the track, he sat hunched in misery. A short distance ahead I also sat down to ease my feet with ointment and put plasters on my blisters. Then we sipped some water and staggered on.

'This is ludicrous,' said Ados. 'I'm giving up. At least I've tried.'

I turned and looked back at him. It was pathetic. All he was trying to do was walk.

'Twenty-five miles a day – it's ridiculous,' he muttered.

'Stop if you want to,' I said. 'But I'm going on. I'll be the fastest man across the Himalayas even if it finishes me!'

At the same time, I knew I couldn't go the full distance alone. Somehow I had to keep my brother with me and hope he grew stronger. Ever since our childhood days

I had always been fitter and faster, challenging family and friends to races. Adrian was the organiser, winning from behind – not by cheating but by bending the rules; by taking alternative routes to the same solution. His were the skills which we needed if we were to survive our plan to become the first men to run the length of the Himalayas. What I couldn't foresee with him spreadeagled in collapse, was that he would not only get up and follow me but go on to take charge. That long before the end of our madcap expedition, he'd be exhorting me, his bigger and stronger brother, to keep going. Nor could I foresee that running the Himalayas would alter the directions of our lives.

Right then I couldn't see beyond Kathmandu. Even if we were fit enough to carry on, events at home could force us to finish the run. And what did it matter? We were only about 2000 miles short of the line!

1

'Let's Make It a Hundred'

THE MOMENT I finished my university research in October 1982, Ados left California and returned to England determined to organise the adventure of his life. He was tired of talking about it and impatient to get something started.

For years he and I had been ticking off challenge after minor challenge without cracking the big one. We'd hitched and biked, run and swum, dived, crawled and climbed, trained and travelled, but our adventuring careers were hardly starspangled. The time had come to attempt something spectacular: but what?

The ground rules were already laid: the expedition had to be organised and completed in a year; it was not to cost more than £5000 (we sold everything we owned except our girlfriends!); it had to be a two-man team trip (because friends and relatives were unable to join in and we, Richard and Adrian Crane, 'definitely' didn't want just any old spare or 'keen' individual!); it had to be exciting for the media and open to sponsorship; and it had to be difficult.

We weren't after money as much as the experience and the satisfaction. Primarily, it was to be a venture towards self-knowledge, a seeking of our limits. Something so challenging that when we failed we could say: 'Well, at least we tried,' and go on to lead more normal lives.

On October 28th, we both went to visit our cousin Nick Crane at Oxford. There, over cups of late night coffee and a map of the world, we went through all the expeditions we could think of – climbing the highest peaks on the earth's seven continents, cycling round the world, walking across the Sahara, hang-gliding off Everest, swimming the Atlantic. But most of our ideas weren't feasible within our rules, had already been done, or were simply too silly.

Then we thought about running . . . and running appealed. It had become a wildly popular sport, and there had to be a distance for us which was not as old-hat as John O'Groats to Land's End, or across the United States. It had to be something like running across Siberia or along the Amazon. What about in some mountains? The Alps, the Rockies, the Himalayas? Yes, from Everest to Kathmandu or K2 to the Indus. How about running the whole length? Of course! 'Running the Himalayas'. What a good idea! It looked 'impossible' enough, and especially so if we were to attempt a traverse in an 'impossible' time. Purely on foot. What a *great* idea! But where do we start and where do we end?

Studying our world map, we came up with a line from Darjeeling (a name we

remembered from our geography books) in India to Everest in Nepal, past Annapurna and over the Tibetan plateau to Rawalpindi in Pakistan. From east to west it
was about 1500 miles, as the plane flies, but on foot and taking into account the
mountainous wiggles, it could be 2500 miles.

We looked at this route and worked out the greatest distance we could possibly
expect to do in optimum conditions for a few consecutive days. This was, we
reckoned from our experience on the British fells, a little over twenty miles a day
which, divided into 2500, gave a race time of one hundred and twenty-five days. We
didn't like the number. It was non-marketable for a start. So we simply said, 'Let's
make it a hundred.'

The fact that we couldn't do it in a hundred days didn't matter because we didn't
expect to reach the end anyway. But it was important to have an eye-catching slogan.
It was also important for the sake of getting started to assure everyone we could do it.
After all, who in their right minds would back a project which was assured of failure!

One of the first things we did after this momentous meeting at Nick's was to
contact a few magazines to see if we could sell an article after the event. The response
was lukewarm. Besides, nobody had ever heard of the Crane brothers. In late
November we began scouting for sponsors – running shoe companies, outdoor
equipment firms and the Royal Geographical Society who turned us down because
they thought our plan was impossible. Nor did other sponsors leap to fund us. Then
one retailer, Cobra Sports Shoe Shop, responded with a modest offer and we were in
business. We even coaxed our friend Vanessa to write a story for the *Reading
Chronicle*. When that appeared with a photograph, it didn't make the Crane Brothers
famous but it gave us encouragement and much-needed backing. At least we had a
press cutting to prove our good intentions.

Meanwhile, we were looking for a purpose outside our own personal satisfaction:
we wanted to team up with a charity. This was not altogether altruistic. While we
would raise money for the charity and publicise its activities, we would also benefit if
adopted by a recognised charity. It would open doors for us, give us respectability
and motivate us to try harder. We had an idea, an expedition and the finance for it.
The charity would organise its own campaign and use all sponsor money for its own
projects. We needed and asked for none. Going through 'The Law Society Gazette of
Charities' we discovered the Intermediate Technology Development Group. The
name was a mouthful but it did just the sort of projects we believed in. It is involved
in Third World aid and self-help programmes which are realistic and mindful of the
cultural values of the people it seeks to raise out of poverty. It was also active in the
Himalayas.

Intermediate Technology (IT from now on) studied the idea, hesitated for a few
weeks then accepted it. 'Go out there and run for us,' they said.

Over New Year, we busied ourselves with an unsuccessful attempt to make a
five-day traverse of the Cuillin Ridge in Skye – something done only a handful of
times in winter, and then in perfect conditions.

On our return, Adrian's girlfriend, Karen Hatfield, arrived from the States and
they went away for a two-week holiday. I was left to organise things but was
interrupted by a three-day panic re-reading of my PhD thesis and preparing for my

viva. With some minor corrections, my work was accepted and the PhD was won. I feel I owe a large part of my perseverance and doggedness on the run to Prof. J. R. L. Allen who taught me the rigours of geological research.

Back from his trip, Adrian helped wrap up the arrangements. We ditched the idea of travelling overland to India because everybody was against it. Instead, we booked with Air India who offered to fly our excess baggage free. Since that weighed 230 pounds, the offer was most helpful.

On the 10th of February, I weighed myself: eleven stone seven pounds. I measured my heartbeat. It was a low fifty-one beats a minute. I was ready to go.

Lord Hunt, whose team conquered Everest in 1953, happily turned out to see us off from the Houses of Parliament though he did warn us that our '. . . time scale is out by a factor of two,' even assuming we escape disease and hypothermia. At Heathrow, the farewell party bubbled on a couple of bottles of champagne and friendship. There was a small gathering of just a few friends and Steve Bonnist, who'd be looking after the IT end and fielding all our reports. Altogether a dozen or so, supplemented by some press and TV South, who filmed us jogging outside on the tarmac.

Then, after handshakes and hugs and a lasting kiss for me from my Michèle, we set off through Passport Control and disappeared into the Departure Hall – the ante room to the skies.

In New Delhi, a British Council representative, Ian Baker, met us at three in the morning. He organised our baggage and ice axes and, with a flick of his British Council card, whisked us through customs to a car that deposited us at a guest house.

At 8.30 I woke up and realised I was actually in India. I counted my heartbeat . . . and counted it again. I couldn't believe it. Then I wrote down 'forty-one beats a minute'.

2

The Run-Up

My PULSE RATE in Delhi didn't reflect what I was feeling. Here's what I wrote at the time:

'What a city! It excites me. Alive with colour and bustle, noise, mess and masses of people, the images are so many and move so fast that I only catch glimpses. Bright yellow scooter taxis hoot and scoot in all directions, their riders jockeying for pole position at the traffic lights. Or avoiding the overflow from the pavements. Colour swarms in front of you, bits and pieces of brightness mixing with the greyer patterns of poverty. Young women with sparkling teeth have gilt bangles and jewels in their noses. A beggary old man squats on his plot of pavement . . . we have reached India.'

Having arrived, it was necessary to explain to the authorities exactly what we were doing and to ascertain what restrictions we faced, what permits we needed to travel through India, Nepal and Pakistan and, in fact, what route we would be allowed to take.

We solicited the aid and advice of Mountain Travel, a leading travel agency in the trekking business, and several Himalayan experts including Commander Kohli, the Indian equivalent of Lord Hunt, who led the successful 1965 Indian Everest expedition.

The Indian officials first had to decide what sort of expedition we were on: mountaineering or trekking. The Home Affairs Ministry said a mountain was anything over 14,000 feet and clearly we would go higher than that. The Indian Mountaineering Foundation, which sanctions all mountain climbs in India, said equally clearly through its director, Mr Motwani, that we weren't on a mountaineering trip and didn't need permits for climbing peaks. In other words, we should be classed as trekkers.

Then there was the question of border crossings. We were told we could either *definitely or possibly* cross the border into Nepal at Simani Basta, Sondali, Tanakpur or Jalabuan. As for guides and porters, we learned certainly we *needed or didn't need* them on certain sections.

The Himachal Pradesh and the Jammu and Kashmir Tourist Offices said we needed special Home Office permission for the Manali-Padum section, but the Ministry of Home Affairs, the Government Tourist Office and Captain Kumar of

Shikhar Travels said we didn't. One official said frankly that to consult the officials only complicated matters. The opinion on the feasibility of the expedition was unanimous, however: all agreed that it was not possible to complete the journey in one hundred days on foot. Even to attempt it was ludicrous.

Very much on the credit side, no one was being obstructive, and we were particularly fortunate in having secured the enthusiastic services of Ms Meher Moos of Air India. She smoothed our way through annoying little hassles and ended up organising a host of 'must-be-dones'.

Another valuable contact we made was Colonel Khullar, the principal of the Himalayan Mountaineering Institute in Darjeeling. We met him at the International Mountaineering Foundation and talked for an hour.

His friendliness and the cooperation he offered for Darjeeling encouraged us to think that our expedition had been accepted by the 'big boys' as a serious attempt. Now we were legitimate Himalayan adventurers.

A week after our arrival, we were impatient to leave Delhi and head for a preparatory workout in the hills. We had, to all intents, worked out our route and the locations of our equipment dumps. We made up several separate packs. Two, with the help of Mountain Travel and Shikhar Travels, were to be forwarded to Srinigar in Kashmir, and Manali in Himachal Pradesh. A third would be left in Kathmandu when we called there en route to Darjeeling and a fourth one in Kausani in Almora district. It was here we headed from Delhi. We had fourteen hours overnight in a crowded, rather ramshackle diesel vehicle which indulged in some hair raising overtaking and heart stopping cornering round countless bends.

As the sun came up, the remarkable country materialised: we were able to see the sheer drops that lurked on the corners and we sought comfort in lifting our eyes to the hills. These grew more and more imposing as we neared Kausani. Indeed, the foothills of Almora were far more precipitous than either of us had imagined. And beyond them we could see for the first time in our lives the frozen peaks of the Himalaya!

Mr K. C. Kunlyar received us warmly into the Hindu religious retreat of Anashakti Ashram, where Mahatma Gandhi had meditated many years ago and Intermediate Technology now had a project.

From the ashram, the view extended clear over the wooded valleys and the terraced hills to the mountains, now ringed with cloud. I listened to the silence and was stirred with good thoughts. In my diary I wrote: 'I can see now why people want to become guru-followers . . . all, everything, absolutely everything, is peaceful, quiet, sunny.'

Then we went running. It was just four months to the day since Adrian had left California to get our act together.

The following morning I woke early, dressed quickly and sprang to see the view again lest it disappear in cloud.

Outside I watched the sky grow lighter and bluer, and the grey valleys turn green again. I felt in love, and wrote to Michèle:

'If you were here, you too could have joined me, slipped quietly out of your cot into the stark-still fresh-chill of the early morning. The sun hasn't risen yet, but the

9

sky is light and from our ashram on a ridge, I can distinguish small villages and their dwellings scattered down below. A pattern of paths links them and their patchwork fields. To the south-east the horizon has an angular edge to it and its ridges are spiked by silhouettes of pin-head trees. But in the other direction, the mountains pierce the clouds . . .'

In the Himalayas, quite clearly, romance rises with the sun.

Adrian also enjoyed this 'acclimatisation' trip, the vistas conjuring up memories of his childhood dreams about climbing in the Himalayas. Soon we had to return to the plains and make for Kathmandu, thirty-six hours away by bus, train and more bus. Two days later we at last arrived on 'the magical plateau of Kathmandu'.

For me it was like arriving in Disneyland, with people of all shapes and sizes in fancy dress, going everywhere at once. There were funny, wonky buildings with intricately carved balconies and overhanging eaves, quaintly decorated temples, bright lights and candles, and tinny transistor radios. Everywhere people were selling things.

The novelty of it all was fascinating, as I recorded it: 'Food comes on a tray with a number of depressions containing rice, greens, chutney and meat curry. It's great: we eat with our fingers, making balls of rice dipped in sauce, and popping them into our mouths. At least that's the idea. We're not very good at it and scatter rice and lentils all over the place. We eat until replete for twelve rupees. That's about sixty English pence!'

On the organisational front, we found Lisa van Gruisen of Tiger Tops Mountain Travel to be fast, friendly, efficient and enthusiastic. She pushed people around to get us our trekking permits, provided us with route information, introduced us to experts and even came up with an invitation from the British Ambassador to attend the annual cricket match between the British and Indian Embassies! Jolly spiffing, what-ho! Sunshine and aperitifs in the pavilion as the morning's play drew to a close. The Indians were 146 for seven after twenty-eight overs.

At lunch we met some of the players: in particular Colonel Mike Allen, the Defence Attaché, who cautioned us gently that the British Embassy was most anxious that we should not do anything illegal. He warned us that there had been severe food shortages in West Nepal, that emergency food drops had been made on a large scale in 1980 and were still being made. Other Nepal experts were even more pessimistic saying 'You won't be able to get any food in West Nepal'. After these sorts of conversations we entered West Nepal fully expecting to have to crawl back out the way we went in.

On the road, we went running with the Hash House Harriers, a club of twenty to thirty ex-patriates who, dressed in a multitude of colours, dashed around the terraces and streams outside Kathmandu. 'Give me more! Give me more!' I exclaimed, feeling strong. As I wrote:

'Running in the sunshine. Phew! It's hot. I fill my clothes with sweat . . . flying along, little kids can't keep up with us and dogs are much less of a problem than we'd anticipated; they, like the cows, are a dozy bunch, only a few have the energy to raise an ear or bat an eyelid.

'Across the river bed, into a village, and up a steep wooded hill. There are steps all the way up, and Buddhist statuettes, stones carved with script, beggars, monks, pious bent old men and women and monkeys!

'We are climbing up to the Monkey Temple, Swayambhunath, with its magnificent white domed stupa, to the red and white prayer flags at the top of the highest hill in the valley of Kathmandu. Sweating profusely, we nearly manage to run all the way and stand gasping as we gaze over the city. No time to rest, we career down the other side to a largish road and go round a loop to re-enter the town. The sun really beats down.'

Our preparation also took us to higher, colder country north of Kathmandu, where we tested our equipment in snow and ice and pushed ourselves up steep, lung-racking, 6000-foot climbs. We were ready.

'We are 12,500 feet up,' I wrote. 'Somewhere between Helambu and Gosainkund, on a rocky ridge. You can practically feel the snow freezing to a crisp as the sunlight dims and the warmth evaporates from our fingers. It's eerie in the evening, windless and oh so silent. Soon we'll lay out our sleeping bags and creep to sleep. Tomorrow we have to turn south again, away from the high mountains that beckon us, back to the valley now bathed in an orange sunset haze. Our trials are nearly over and our trial will soon begin.

3

Kanchenjunga to Nanga Parbat

FROM KATHMANDU to Darjeeling by bus is a nightmare. It's the sort of journey that is hell at the time but you wouldn't have missed for the world once it's over.

We caught the six pm Saturday 'Rocket', an overnight express bus which takes you to the Nepalese border. From there you take another bus to Siliguri, a city on the northern plains of India and only another lurch or two up to Darjeeling. Each stage is an exercise in passenger endurance.

The Nepalese bus is closely related to its ramshackle smoking cousins found in other Third World countries – South America, East Africa, India. But the Nepalis have refined the art of creating discomfort by insisting on the mistaken arithmetical calculation that six bums into four seats will go. They've also reduced any interior luggage space to an absolute minimum by blocking up the space under the seats. This means you have to sit with all your valuables on your lap all night. Not only that, they let the aisles fill up with standers. Is that all? No, they've raised part of the floor of the bus and lowered the roof so the standers must bend, so you're quite likely to be cheek-to-cheek with someone else's backside.

When the bus is full, they invite more people on board – and only then does the driver crash into gear and surge forward, one hand on the horn and the other on the wheel. A gang of youths bang on the sides of the bus, yell and scream every time they see a corner or another vehicle coming, or a person in the road. In addition, a loudspeaker screeches, the diesel engine fumes underneath you, and the brakes shriek in surprise every time the driver's danger reflexes make him thump the brake pedal.

Add to all this the shakes, rattles and rolls and the fact that it is stifling, dusty and exceedingly arm-pitty and you have fifteen hours of one of the most diabolical bus rides ever time-tabled. Even when the boys get tired of their bus-bashing and succumb to boredom, the bus itself has reserves of energy to keep its assault on the senses going all night. I didn't sleep a wink.

Midday in Siliguri was sweltering. We climbed into a taxi of Morris Minor vintage while the driver waited for a full complement of passengers. The fare to Darjeeling for the two and a half hour, sixty kilometre trip was twenty-five rupees, £1.25 sterling, and it seemed that there weren't that many people in a hurry to do the journey. So we sat and roasted.

Our taxi driver came to life once we hit 'Darj City'. Suddenly he was a bundle of

fun, humping our rucksacks and laughing under their weight. He was also posses-
sive, kicking out at other taxi drivers and hotel touts who saw us as likely custom.
With a broad smile he asked for double fare. I smiled broadly back.

Darjeeling struck me as a fantasy place, a toy-town, with steep streets and brightly
painted wooden houses. From an elevated view above the town, its bazaar was as
colourful as a cardboard cut-out. Darjeeling was also run down and poor, though. In
the street a fuzzy haired beggar in fluttering rags and bare feet offered a toothless
grin and his empty palm. His eyes were fixed on the sky. He was disconcerting, and
eventually he went off dancing down the road . . .

When Tenzing Norgay, the most famous Sherpa of them all, slipped away from his
Himalayan home and went to Darjeeling, the town in 1932 was a place of wonder. At
the bottom of the steep hill on which it had grown was the cosmopolitan old part
with its many people – Nepalis, Tibetans, Bhutanese, Sherpas and Hindus –
crowding the narrow streets and bazaars. The newer part of the city, overlooking the
old, was even more fascinating. Here were the big homes of the officers of the British
Empire, the tea company officials and the richer Indians. The streets had fine stores
and tea houses, even a movie theatre. But there were even grander buildings –
Government House, the summer residence of the Governor of Bengal, a maharaja's
palace and a hotel 'like a castle'. Behind them, the great Himalayas.

On the Kali Gandhaki in central Nepal, for instance, the valley floor lies at 4000
feet. Rising over 20,000 feet above it in a gigantic mass to a height of 26,800 feet is
Dhaulagiri. Across the valley rears Annapurna: nowhere else on earth does the
vertical rise so sharply, so stupendously. Even the foothills would be classed as
mountain ranges if they were situated elsewhere. They were formed in an incredible continental collision which started many millions of years ago and is still
going on slowly today. Along a front of 1700 miles the impact forced the land masses
upwards and fourteen peaks now stand higher than any others in the world at over
8000 metres above the sea. In time these peaks were given names like Kangchenjunga, Makalu, Dhaulagiri, Annapurna, Nanga Parbat and Chomolungma, 'Goddess
Mother of the World', the mountain 'so high no bird can fly over it'.

For the people who lived in their shadow they represented the home of the Gods,
the eternal background to people's everyday struggle to survive. When the Europeans came with their curiosity and measuring sticks, they rendered the mountains
more accessible: to the explorers and adventurers (mostly British) who wished to
enlarge the boundaries of science or who sought to test themselves against the
unknown, do the spectacular or heroic or record making thing. For the sake of King
and country – and, of course, for fame and sometimes fortune.

We were curious in a scientific way about how our bodies and mental spirit would
cope with our trial of endurance. We also had the Union Jack behind us though we
preferred to wave the flag of Intermediate Technology. And our family and friends
wanted us to try our hardest.

Would we be able to accomplish the first complete traverse on foot?

The early explorers, then much later the surveyors and sportsmen, probed and

13

plotted their way from one great mountain to another. The combined total of their footsteps had, to all intents, covered the length and breadth of the ranges. But no recorded expedition had ever set out to run along the whole length in a foolhardy race against time. And certainly not on a shoestring operation like ours. We were like no previous expedition.

In 1980, for example, an Indian Army team set out from Arunchal Pradesh in India's north-east corner and, after one and a half to two years of travel along a high mountain route, they finished their journey just north of Leh in the Ladakh region of the Karakorams. This was about 200 miles short of Nanga Parbat, the most eastern of the great peaks.

Theirs was very much an official, 'big team' expedition, with all the back-up necessary. It progressed stoically in 'relay' fashion and possibly no one member stayed with the expedition for the full course.

In 1981 Peter Hillary, whose father had conquered Everest with Tenzing, teamed up with Graham Dingle, another New Zealander, and Chewang Tashi, a Sherpa guide and nimble linguist. They started in Sikkim with a support team of four, two of whom joined in parts of the traverse. From Darjeeling they took a bus into Nepal where they started their hike to Lamayuru in Ladakh. From here, they hitched a lift to Leh, and flew via Delhi and Rawalpindi back to K2, the world's second highest mountain, in Pakistan, where their journey ended. They stayed high most of the time, crossing many snow passes. They took ten months.

The experts might say they tackled the thing wisely, with the right amount of support and taking a reasonable amount of time. As far as we were concerned, it was just a very long and leisurely trek, not an adventure to stretch body and mind. Or make the headlines.

In 1980–81, two Americans, Hugh Swift and Arlene Blum, started a trek from Bhutan and, a year later, finished in Lamayuru inside India. This team rode buses in some places and employed mountain guides and porters.

The latest traverse team, calling itself the British Women's Trans-Himalayan Expedition, were following the same precedents, busing where they thought it necessary and employing guides and porters. This team had set off from Sikkim in January '83 and was hundreds of miles ahead by the time we reached Darjeeling. In fact we had met a friendly Pam Tubby, one of the expedition members, on our visit to Kathmandu where she was recovering from frost bite. Her partner, Elaine Brooks, had gone on ahead.

Despite the women's head-start and our decision not to touch transport, we calculated on overtaking our rivals. After all, we'd be travelling super-light. One rucksack, one sleeping bag, one set of clothes, one pair of shoes, and shared between us: map, diaries, camera, penknife, water jar and two plastic teaspoons. No guides, no porters, no shelter, no food, no water. And we would be running. Looked at logically, the idea was preposterous.

'You should allow twice as much time,' Lord Hunt had told us.

'You'll end up crawling,' said Captain Kohli.

'You're going to what?!' exclaimed the reporter from the *Cumberland News and Star*.

At the time we weren't sure of our geography. It was only later in the journey that we realised the route from Kanchenjunga, past all fourteen 8000-metre peaks, to Nanga Parbat in Pakistan represented a true and definable traverse. This would become our target. By starting in Darjeeling, just east of the mountain, we could quickly tick off Kanchenjunga.

4

Departure From Darjeeling

DILIP, THE COOK at the Himalayan Mountaineering Institute, was perplexed. He'd come to our room carrying in cups of 'bed tea' and to ask us what time we'd be wanting breakfast. I said at nine. And then, if it wasn't too much bother, lunch at ten.

'It's called carbo-loading,' said Ados, rather enjoying the man's bemused reaction.

'We don't know where our next meal is coming from,' I added, equally mischievous.

'You go today?' asked Dilip.

He couldn't seem to make us out and it wasn't surprising. We hardly resembled the usual adventurers who stayed at the Himalayan Mountaineering Institute. We had none of the climbers' paraphernalia: mountain boots, tents, ice axes or ropes. And we obviously weren't trekkers. Nor tourists.

'Yes, Dilip, we're off. At twelve o'clock.'

The cook nodded and stood there watching us as we pushed the guest room furniture aside, put on our Gore-Tex weathersuits, gloves and balaclavas, and wriggled into our sleeping bags.

'Just testing,' I explained. Then to impress him I reached for the needle and thread to sew up the slit left in my duvet jacket by the removal of its metal duvet poppers. Ados stood up, bent over, and with a flourish cut six inches off his shoe laces.

'They're too heavy, Dilip. Too long, too heavy,' he said. 'And look, even labels.' He showed the Indian a bag of superfluous labels, buttons, poppers and cuffs that we'd snipped off our brand new equipment to reduce our load. We'd actually got our packs down to 5.3 kilograms each. That's 11½ pounds. Several pounds less than our early estimates.

'Ah. You flying. By aircraft?' Dilip grinned with understanding but he frowned again when I said:

'No, we're going on foot. All the way.'

Dilip wanted to know where our porters were; how many we were using; did we have other friends; and what about food and packs and extra clothing.

We told him there were only the two of us, that we didn't need spare clothes, and we would pick up fresh equipment along the way. As for food, we would find that where we could. If necessary, we would live on fresh air. In fact, we felt so high we could probably run on it too.

It was not only our expectations and adrenalin that pumped out optimism. Getting started was an achievement in itself. We had overcome our own doubts, cut through bureaucratic red tape and, in fact, were chuffed with the cheeky way we'd organised things. Compared with other ambitious adventures, ours was practically an 'instant' expedition. And here we were on schedule. We'd chalk up Kanchenjunga, the first of the great 8000-metre peaks on the very first day, and we were raring to go.

When Dilip left us, I looked at my brother. He was smiling broadly. I started a giggle that got uncontrollable and in moments we were both tumbling about with laughter.

We couldn't have been more pleased with ourselves.

At midday Colonel Khullar, our host and director of the Mountaineering Institute, was waiting for us in his office. A delightful man, he was the first, really the only mountaineering person of standing who greeted our plans with spontaneous encouragement, and we were grateful for this. With him was a small contingent of the press and the one and only Tenzing Norgay. He was immediately recognisable from those faded photos of his shining, smiling face at Edmund Hillary's shoulder. But that was thirty years before and, at 69 years, he looked smaller as well as older than the hero of the Himalayas I had imagined. He wore a flat cap – and an expression that suggested he had already sized us up. And we didn't amount to much. With our running shoes and mini-sized packs we must have looked like cocky upstarts compared with the long line of great adventurers who had reached peaks with him.

There's little doubt he was doing us a favour being there, for his name still impressed news editors and illuminated a piece in the papers. Certainly his presence gave us more credibility and we appreciated him for that. But he himself, like so many others, didn't believe we could run anywhere in the Himalayas let alone along it in 100 days. We went on insisting it could be done, if not by us, by someone, someday.

Unfortunately, we really didn't have time to talk, which is difficult anyway when you're being pushed, as we were, into poses for pictures. We also had to wrap up the formalities. We got Tenzing and Colonel Khullar to sign our log book, and the colonel was typically generous. For the record he wrote: 'Midday 18 March 1984. A unique honour for us at the HMI that the enterprising Crane brothers begin their great venture here. Wishing them a smooth and a very interesting run and God Bless.'

Ados gave a card and an IT running singlet to the colonel for his institute's collection. Mrs Bathachaya of the Darjeeling Tourist Office presented us with scarves, photographers took more pictures, and a few words of farewell were spoken. Then suddenly all that was left were the handshakes.

I think both of us were pretending to be a bit blasé about the whole thing, as though this sort of mammoth marathon was a doddle for us. But people cried: 'Good luck! Good luck!' and as they waved us away, I think I must have caught a whiff of fame. Whatever it was, I must confess I felt rather special inside and, as we ran down the Tenzing Norgay Road, out of Darjeeling, it put an extra spring in my step.

This high-spirit fuel carried us quickly over the first few miles. I thought of Michèle back home. We had started the run on March 18th because that is her birthday. What

17

better reason to choose a day could we want? I carried her photograph, trimmed for weight, in my pack and I was already longing to see her again. But nothing detracted from the delight at actually being on the road. My brother and I.

We told each other how fit we felt, and how marvellously light our 11½ pound rucksacks were. We argued over who carried the better-packed load and noted how the mist came curling down to cover the hills. We ran, lightly, through the village of Ghoom and into the mist that obliterated the view and seeped through to our sweat. But I was in my element.

Some way out, we stopped. A road sign claimed: 'Slow and steady wins the race', and we took a photograph of ourselves, laughing, beside it.

We pulled into a chai house festooned with noodles and photos from Chinese and Indian magazines. The sweet tea we expected turned out to be Tibetan – a gagging mix of salt and rancid butter. Ados slung his out the window. Then on, down the steep mountain spurs. It was all so effortless, side-stepping the other people on the trail, the dogs and horses and a bullock cart. For a while we allowed a group of school-children to keep up with us, humouring them with answers for their curiosity; then we slipped into overdrive and glided out of sight. We even imagined we were skiers: leaning into the hillside, our speed carried us in a wide line round the bends and we hardly slowed when we hit the rough verges. We would be unstoppable!

We did twenty-one miles that first afternoon, and stopped for the night at the Hotel Shyam in Kurseong. It was a bit too comfortable for the masochist in me and a little pricey by Indian standards but, what the hell, it was our first night and we had a lot of hardship to look forward to. Besides we could afford it, for we carried about £200 of rupees with us, hidden away in our packs. More than enough to raise a fear of bandits. However, we weren't going to let that worry us, and when we totted up the day's events we were rich in credit. But our euphoria had evaporated.

5

Sisyphus and Super One-Upman

THE EUPHORIA was mostly mine. And as infectious as it might have been, it was not fully shared by Adrian. He still couldn't comprehend with any satisfaction what we were aiming to accomplish. The idea of reaching Rawalpindi was too far-fetched to be a tangible goal. Indeed, the picture of running and running and running into the future was more than both our minds could see. How can anyone conceive a distance beyond their experience? Our tactics were simply to run one day at a time.

Adrian also showed early signs of suffering. That very first afternoon he derived no pleasure from running in the mist, and he muttered about the cold which made him shiver. The stop for tea, which had turned out to be Tibetan, had nearly made him sick. What's more, he experienced the first niggles of his natural impatience which, combined with his ideas on energy conservation, would make problems between us. His diary the next morning made plain his complaint:

'Nearly 7 am. Waiting in the teahouse for Dick to come from the room after fooling with his shoe soles. Ten minutes he said. This is such a bore, waiting and waiting for him. Today is an easy day so I shall not nag him but I hate this time wasting. I could save a lot of energy walking on ahead instead of pissing about here, then running. I hope this is an isolated case. He may be better when he gets rid of his sewing kit. Let's just get on with this thing!'

This summed up Adrian's attitude. It wasn't a fun run we were on and the sooner we finished it the better. He objected to my being too methodical, too precise about everything – tying my shoelaces again and again, repacking my gear, writing my diary, fiddling with this or that, adjusting my pack and not setting off until everything was exactly right.

Adrian expanded later 'The basic problem is that Richard's a stubborn perfectionist. He always has to do things thoroughly and properly. It's nothing new. Even as a small boy he scrupulously followed the instructions when playing with our Meccano set. He painted his plastic models meticulously, always using the correct colours. He was equally conscientious about his homework, tackling it each and every day after an afternoon snack of exactly one-and-a-half slices of toast with peanut butter and bovril.'

Young Adrian had a far more easy-going attitude to life. He was, for instance, haphazard in his snacking habits, eating if and when a bite was going. Much to my seething irritation, he was slap-dash with his models. He painted them with

19

abandon whatever colour his whim chose. He also supplemented his Meccano pieces with bits of wood and wire to create novel models of his own.

Adrian has a more adventurous personality, a more inquisitive mind. As far as homework was concerned, that more often than not was done in a rush, the next day, at school. He worked at being the casual individual, showing all the symptoms of one-upmanship, surprising his teachers and peers by achieving with little apparent effort. He reckons he's got the balance between work and play just right, and has developed a philosophical shrug to cope with pressures and disappointment. He is also capable of turning his back on obstacles that bore him or that he regards as being beneath effort.

His technique in life is to take the short cut, and if there isn't one, he's got his shrug to fall back on.

Our Dad says I'm more dogged. In my desire to do things thoroughly, I miss the short cuts and I drive myself on willpower. I just have to overcome the insurmountable, no matter how painful the attempt. Suffering is acceptable, surrender unthinkable, and success is what it's all about. Failure would be a sign of inadequacy. Consequently, I suppose I have a need to prove myself. Michèle says I suffer from the Sisyphus syndrome: there's always another boulder for me to shove up the mountain. Another work load of worry.

Mum always said that I'm a terrier with detail, doubt and worry. She said that if I had someting on my mind then it nags there, I can't let it go. Not until I've wrestled it to submission, run it into the ground, or squashed it into pulp. I suppose this sort-of head-down perseverance hasn't made life any easier for me. This explains why Ados, free of worries, invariably slept better than me. It was a significant advantage that, later in the expedition, would have a bearing on our performance.

On the evening of our second day, we had crossed our first border. My diary says:

'We made Karkavitta just inside Nepal by sundown. Ace! We took it fairly easy from Kurseong – all day for thirty miles – but it wasn't all that comfortable. Thirty miles out of Darjeeling we were still up in the hills and soaked by the cold mist which had Ados muttering. Then, not much later and nearer the border, we hit the plains and the Hell-heat. The countryside 1000 feet above sea level was dead flat; set about with bamboo clumps and plump banana plants. We ran with sweat, fanned by a wind that came from a furnace. We warned ourselves to beware of heat exhaustion. But I was thinking more of Ados, because his complexion grills easily. I also detect he's getting a bit hot under the collar over my sewing. I'll humour him and finish it.'

In fact we did not work particularly hard at humouring each other. Nor did we make emotional demands. We never had. Not the way you'd perhaps try to please friends, or be obliged to people outside the family. We'd simply always taken our relationship for granted, and despite our many years of brotherliness, we'd never been very close. Now, however, we were living every intimate minute together. And one way or the other this was bound to affect our feelings for one another. The run was to become a major test of our compatibility. But whatever happened we'd still be brothers.

One of the basic ground rules in our partnership was that each should do his bit. We were determined to split the burden equally and fairly, and this led to serious

Dick (*left*), Ados (*right*), on 18 March 1983 outside the Himalayan Mountaineering Institute, Darjeeling, about to start their epic run.

Little school-kids submerge us. *Day 2. Nepalese foothills.*

Ados forces his way up the crowded main street of Chainpur past ladies carrying firewood.

Ados leads Dick up to a 10,000 ft pass with mani (prayer) stones. *Day 8. East Nepal.*

Dick massaging his feet and washing his socks in an icy stream at dusk at Dughla (15,150 ft) below Everest Base Camp. *Day 12.*

Ados running up to a Buddhist chorten on the trail towards Ama Dablam. *Day 12.*

Ados scorches round a corner early in the journey.

Dick (*left*), Ados (*behind*) enjoying a moment's respite at 15,000 ft near Everest Base Camp.

Dick leads Ados across a bridge on the route down to Kathmandu from Everest Base Camp. *Day 17.*

Margaret Percy (Radio 4) interviews Ados in Kathmandu after the record-breaking run from Everest Base Camp. *Day 18.*

Hustle and bustle in Kathmandu. *Day 18.*

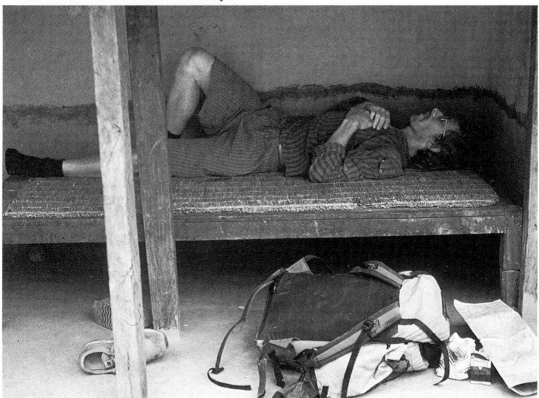

Adrian flat on his back at Sallentar with dysentery and heat exhaustion. *Day 24.*

Ados (*left*), Dick (*right*), at 13,000 ft in front of Dhaulagiri. *Day 34.*

discussions, for example, on the weight of our respective packs. Because Adrian was smaller and weighed less, we wondered if the pack weight should be distributed proportionately. In other words, if I should carry somewhat more than Adrian. But my younger brother's pride wouldn't allow that. In the event, we decided the weight distribution was fair as it was because my personal gear was slightly heavier than Adrian's: 'He had larger shoes for one thing,' says Adrian. 'And he wrote more diaries!'

This was not a joke. I now realise after the run that I wrote reams, reporting names and details with the fervour of a scientist. Adrian, on the other hand, did what he thought was enough, the minimum, and not just because he knew that I would get it all. He was satisfied with one understated, capsulated entry a day. The pages from my school exercise books, datelined by the hour, are evidence that I hauled out my paperwork practically every time we stopped.

Where Adrian was cryptic, I was expansive. According to my diary, we set out from Karkavitta to Ilam and went 'from the absurd to the ridiculous'. We 'fought buses' on the East-West highway. We got lost, 'ploughed through a dirt bowl', 'disrupted a local primary school', 'bashed up hills', 'struggled over dry river beds' and were 'hit by a tropical downpour'. All in one day!

We jogged in stifling heat and I was struck by how still the countryside was. It was like being in the middle of a slow-motion movie and not the 'active throbbing India' I'd always imagined. Here everything 'seemed stunned, sleepy men eyed us lazily, buffaloes could barely spare the effort to flick away their flies, the birds were muted and the breeze held its breath.'

We stumbled across a dry river bed and along a grass track towards a green pasture when a mass of children, uniformed in white, blue and grey, erupted out of a school and came pouring towards us yelling and whooping. My first instinct was to turn and run away but we ploughed on until we were submerged by a couple of hundred of the little beasties.

The children, here and elsewhere, seemed to regard us as some sort of travelling entertainment and often swarmed around us chattering and squealing. Practising their meagre English, they would cry: 'Hello', 'Goodbye', 'Tell me name', and they'd jump up and down, pushing each other and pulling faces.

From a teahouse we bashed on over a 700 foot pass in dense jungle, crossed another dry river bed and hacked through a very English beech forest, its floor piled thick with fallen leaves. Following an old disused cart track, we made our way on to darkness and found ourselves in Chisapani. Here I estimated we'd covered something more than thirty-five miles of obstacles that day, including about 3000 feet of climbing. We had been so slow about it that it made me feel decidedly expletive. According to my diary:

'What a way to spend a day! When someone in the next few years reads that two knackers, attempting a fast traverse of the Himalayas, took a whole day to go from Karkavitta to Chisapani, they'll say "Bloody hell! No wonder the buggers didn't get far!" '

Adrian, on the other hand, thought it had been a 'neat' day but 'perhaps we pushed ourselves a bit hard'.

21

In Chisapani we met a VSO volunteer who hadn't spoken English for a month. He was apparently totally wrapped up in his job and did not want to meet 'foreigners', though we persuaded him to let us sleep on his floor.

The fact was, if we were going to get anywhere by 'living off the land' or, rather, 'living off the people who lived off the land', we couldn't afford to be coy and diffident or too polite. We were determined to enjoy hospitality, if necessary before it was offered, and to ignore any signs or hints that we weren't really welcome. Which is probably what the VSO worker was trying to tell us. We rationalised this single-minded approach to overnight accommodation rather simply:

In the first place, it was unlikely that people would turn away two weary travellers in search of food and shelter. The more remote people were, the greater would be their willingness to be hospitable. Since most of our stopovers would be off the tourist and commercial track, in places foreigners seldom appeared, the locals would be only too delighted to receive us.

Armed with this attitude and, on occasion, with a degree of desperation, we were even prepared to enter homes without invitation. We reasoned that if we stood outside and knocked or called and waited, we would be taken in sooner or later. We just preferred it to be sooner.

'Besides,' says Adrian, 'we knew so little of the local culture that whatever we did could be wrong, and frankly I don't think we took undue advantage of the people. We never took the food out of anyone's mouth. We always offered them money to compensate them and they invariably made us welcome.'

Our main fears were accidents and injury on the isolated sections of our route; the possibility that we might get lost, or suffer exposure in the cold at high altitudes and heat stroke in the valleys. There was also the fear that aches and blisters might escalate into serious ailments; that we'd be overcome by dehydration and exhaustion; fall prey to the nasty microbes that lived in food and water – or the germs of weakness in our personalities that could undermine our will to go on.

We took precautions, of course. We carried medical tips written out on a piece of airmail paper and a minimum supply of medicines – antibiotics for dysentery, bits of elastoplast for blisters, iodine tablets to purify any unboiled water. For a while we also carried a piece of string!

We kept a close check on our physical condition, not merely as a precaution but out of scientific curiosity. We regularly measured our heartbeats; checked the consistency of our stools and noted the amounts of liquid we drank and how much we urinated. On the way to Chisapani, I had drunk six litres of liquid and only pissed out half a litre.

Whenever possible we ate fruit and vegetables that we could peel ourselves and food that we had seen prepared and cooked. We sterilised all our drinking water with tablets. We each had our individual plastic teaspoon, and for lightness Adrian drilled holes in the handle of his! But the way we were travelling it was impossible to be scrupulous in our eating habits. It was all a gamble. But, being the Crane brothers, we called it calculated. And as we completed the run from Chisapani to Ilam, and on to Roxi, northwards towards the high mountains, our major complaint was that it was still such a bloody long way.

6

'Namaste'

KURSEONG, KARKAVITTA, Chisapani, Roxi, Moktara and Taplejung – the number of nightstop names we could drop was mounting behind us. About four nights ahead lay Lukla, only a hop and a skip from Everest, with its airfield and promise of news from home. It was something to look forward to.

On the road to Taplejung we were diverted by people streaming up a steep path to Nohme Bazar, a twice-a-month market atop a ridge. Most of them were women with lovely big eyes and fine features. They wore bright saris and flowery headscarves, rings in their ears and noses. Curious, we followed and dawdled for a while in the middle of all their marketing and merchandising.

From Nohme Bazar, we dropped to the river, ran past rice paddies, then steeply up again to 5000 feet and above, where the cultivated terraces gave way to sheer rock. But Taplejung was elusive. We spent hours cornering hill after hill until at last our faith that Taplejung was just around the next hill was rewarded.

In Norgay's Guest House (seventy-six rupees for dinner, bed and breakfast) I totted up the day's physical cost. I had a sore instep, a heat rash on my back and a complaining knee joint. Then came a dreadful night. I was woken at 1.30 by a barking mastiff chained below our window. I got dressed, lit a wick lamp and put in my contact lenses and determined to go and stone that dog to death. Thought better of it but swore viciously and took my sleeping bag into another room, away from the barking, and went to sleep on a table. At five the house started rousing and I went back to our room. Ados was still asleep. He said he hadn't heard the dog. I think he could sleep through World War Three.

To him, his sleeping bag was 'this luxurious cocoon of warmth', and he hated getting up, especially to climb into 'horrible dust-encrusted clothes' and socks as stiff as plaster casts. I'd had a go at washing my socks the night before, but they were still miserably wet and cold when we set off.

From Taplejung we bashed up 8000 feet, leaving village habitation below and behind. We groped our way through misty forests at 10,000 feet, and when dusk fell, stumbled down a rocky trail. We were well into the eerie moonlight and wondering about a night in the open when we ran into signs of life. Not bothered where we stayed, we walked to the door of the first hut we came to.

'Namaste,' I called. We waited.

A young man, barefooted, in grey woollen shorts, and smock came out.

'Namaste,' we said again, warmly, and put the palms of our hands together to emphasise the politeness of our greeting. We couldn't see his reaction properly in the dark but I bet his expression was quizzical.

'Pani,' I said. 'Ek cup pani dinus – Water, please give us a cup of water.' The man seemed to understand and as he stepped back inside, we stooped and quickly followed him through the opening.

We found ourselves in a dark and smoky windowless room – the whole dwelling – and tried to focus. There were two central wooden pillars holding up the loft and roof. Just off centre there was a two-foot-square hearth with a fire that flickered weakly. The only other source of measly light was a petrol wick lamp. There were reed baskets, wooden tubs, cooking bowls and an assortment of sticks and poles around the walls.

Faces that turned out to be two little boys and their mother peered at us from the gloom. Draped in layers of cloth, her feet tucked away, the woman resembled a pile of dirty clothing beside the fire. She spoke to her husband in unintelligible sounds, to which he answered as incomprehensibly.

The man pulled a reed mat across the floor and we assumed it was meant for us. We sank onto it, making our own language noises and puffing them out with gratitude.

'We'd better tell them we're hungry,' said Ados. 'That we also want food.'

'And how do you say "if you don't mind we have no intention of leaving?" ' I asked darkly.

Mustering our few phrases and mixing them with a mime, we persuaded the couple that we were harmless, friendly and hungry. They offered us food and we hoped that they'd let us stay the night. Further attempts at conversation proved pointless and anyway with a warm fire and good friends one doesn't have to talk. We all sat silently staring into the fire.

We did, however, ascertain what a three-foot-high tub was doing balanced on a set of hearthstones – the man was brewing up an alcoholic potion which turned out to be home-made rakshi. Made from corn, it is the local equivalent of whisky. It was drinkable, so we bought a dishful when it was ready. It made Ados feel warm. I got quite drunk.

Meanwhile, the woman had been preparing our meal. She spent some time in the firelight, separating dahl lentils from the chaff with the flick of her fingers. Then she ground them on a circular stone grinder which fed their powdered form onto the clay floor. This was then swept up in her hand and put into a pot. While she cooked the rice, the man put his talent for alchemy to mixing the dahl with an oniony sauce.

By this time Ados and I were ravenous but our wait was worthwhile. We had the best dahl bhaat we'd tasted, followed by corn they popped for desert. It was an excellent meal, helped by the ambience. More than Ados, I was into the 'ethnic' side of our expedition, and I couldn't have wished for a more ethnic experience than this. In their warm if smoky, far-from-anywhere home, I felt I was meeting the real people.

Not long after the meal, the woman lay down beside the fire alongside her children. We took that as the cue for bed and went outside to sleep under the lean-to

24

wood store. I woke once to look at the stars and moon but otherwise slept soundly until a rooster started his crowing claim that he was cock of the walk.

At 6.40 we were up and running, with Ados wanting to know why it took us so long. I think his irritation was partly due to the fact that he wasn't enjoying the adventure. His diary entries at the time contain strong hints of homesickness (or, if you prefer, lovesickness) and defeatism.

On Day 6, for instance, Ados was wondering 'how far I can get on these aching legs . . . the cold and mist really get to me . . .'

The next day he was complaining about more 'damn photographs', and feeling his hamstring. What's more, he tripped as we approached Chainpur and went sliding down the path, skinning his knee and elbow. It was an alarming thing to do, especially since one moment of carelessness could end the whole thing.

He was irritated with some 'poor route finding', as I was. It was not only a waste of time and energy, it also sapped our morale and, as he said, undermined his willpower. So he was 'dispirited' as we arrived in Tumlingtar where we found a cheap hostel – seventeen rupees for dinner and bed for two. Here Ados went through his bits and pieces and re-read a letter from Karen. He sighed into his diary:

'It's so lovely to think of her and my return.'

Such moments of longing (I certainly had my own) made us wish like hell it was all over, but they also reinforced our resolve to carry on by reminding us of all the people we were running for, family, friends and the charity Intermediate Technology. We didn't want to disappoint them. Nevertheless, after one hundred and eighty miles and one week, Ados was confiding:

'The thought of failure does not worry me. I'd be quite happy with an early retirement! Go to the US and take things easy.'

Then he was going on about the home delights of Maryport buns and marmalade and as much tea as he could drink. And Karen again. On Day 8, he couldn't 'bear' to contemplate ninety-two more days, or having to take the lead in certain sections.

'I seem to have just run out of energy,' he wrote. And if this weren't bad enough, he added: 'I've had thoughts today of seriously twisting my ankle and being able to stop at last . . . all I want to do is get out of the place.'

By now we were nearly nine days into high adventure, and we had left Nundhaki, Chainpur, Tumlingtar behind. The eleven-hour haul to the Rai village of Phedi was a particularly memorable day. We set out from Tumlingtar, crossed the plains of the Arun valley and were ferried across the big river in a dugout canoe. Safely across, we made our own route up the other side, clambering up a boulder-strewn hill to the west side terraces.

In a reed hut we drank soupy millet beer and ate a dish of ground rice and yoghurt, then ran again: down into steamy jungle and up river banks and cliffs on paths so narrow, steep and slippery that back home they'd be wired off and labelled 'Danger, Beware!'

We found another haat bazar where we bought greasy dough rings and bananas and had another go at the millet beer. Then off we went, threading our way through a narrow belt of rice paddies at the bottom of the Irkwa Khola gorge. Since starting out from Darjeeling, we'd crossed any number of bridges – metal and wooden suspension bridges, wooden rampart bridges, bamboo tension bridges, single bamboo ramps, wooden logs and stepping stones. We met a variety of shaky bridges this day as we crossed and recrossed this tributary of the Arun before climbing up the mountainside to reach Phedi by moonlight.

Here we took pot luck again. This time with a Sherpa family, a couple with five children. I was overjoyed that we were actually feeling the pulse of Nepal.

7

A Climb to Sorrow

ONE COMPENSATION in arriving at a village after dark was the revelation of the morning. Immense vistas blacked out by the night developed gradually from first light, like photographs, into fabulous views: mountains, ravines, terraces and valleys.

We had to get up and reduce all those wonderful panoramas to the level of a footslog. Put one foot in front of the other – and watch where we were putting it. This was easier for me than for Ados. I could switch off. But he suffered from boredom which aggravated his complaints.

Looking back, there were a number of clues pointing to our creeping weariness. But nothing was as pointed as our obsession with the weight of our load. The packs we'd once regarded as lightweight had grown heavier in spite of shedding every superfluous ounce. We abandoned the idea of ever carrying any food, partly because we were buying or cadging enough to sustain us and partly because we would notch up another victory, another first, if we completed a Himalayan journey without any supplies. So we even got rid of the plastic bag we had carried in case we needed to get any emergency rations.

We shed yet more. Our sawn-off toothbrush we threw with some ceremony into the Arun river. We tore off, with some satisfaction, large areas of our maps as we left places behind. We gave away one plastic beaker, only keeping the other because we'd discovered that we often had to have our own cup when buying drinks.

We could not gauge the effect of all this weight reduction. But one thing is certain – even carrying nothing we'd have been exhausted by the time we reached Bung, a large and typical Rai mountain village. The long ascent from the Honga Khola river, which you cross on the most rickety of bridges, was a real bastard. At the end of it we were washed out and in dire need of a pint of water, a pile of rice and a level place to collapse for the night.

Somewhere in the middle part of Bung we came across a merry party of porters who, to our surprise and delight, were waiting on fourteen representatives of the British Army – more particularly the Cheshire Regiments' Himalayan Acorns climbing expedition – and the first foreigners we'd met for days.

We set about making instant friends. The result was that we were able to get stuck into their cold leftovers – pots of boiled and mashed potato, rice, dahl and, wonder of wonders, a tin of bully beef – all washed down with large mugs of hot tea.

27

'You're a hungry couple of buggers,' said one of the soldiers.

For a couple of hours we relaxed into swopping stories of home, of climbing, motor cars and girlfriends. In our log book they wrote, 'Entertained Richard and Adrian to dinner – the remains of our food. They obviously hadn't had a decent meal for some time. We wish them well, but to a man we are glad not to be going with them.'

The climbers did more than feed us. They also helped recharge our batteries. We woke refreshed and excited. It was Day 10, and we wanted to reach Lukla that day. Beyond Lukla we could actually start visualising Everest!

For the first time, we realised we were really getting somewhere. We'd actually reached the threshold of one of the most wildly romantic areas in the world! We were so buoyant we felt we could bounce over the obstacles to Lukla. To make it easier still, we abandoned our mug in Bung, leaving only a plastic container for water.

We made light of the next two 10,000 foot passes we came to and bounded on to the valley of the 'Milky River', the Dudh Kosi, which flows from its many tributaries in the Everest massif through the Solo Khumbu, the heartland of the high-climbing Sherpas!

For centuries this part of Nepal was remote and primitive, peopled by hardy tribes and closed to foreigners. The deep river valleys and steep trails that edged along gorges were the main trade route to the south. To the north lay the main spiritual path to holy Tibet – the ancestral home of the Sherpa, on the other side of Chomolungma. After the Second World War, Nepal, which can boast that it has never been conquered, opened its borders and let the adventurers in.

They came in a trickle at first: mountaineers in search of the path to the top of Mount Everest. Since it was climbed in 1953, the few have become a flood and Solo Khumbu today is Trekker Territory. When Tenzing Norgay was a boy, and indeed even after he'd become famous, the remarkable yak was the Sherpa's 'great staple of life'. Now it is the tourist. They fly into Lukla and Kathmandu by the load to trudge in the steps of the mountain guides and breath the same rare air. Few, however, approach the mountains via the back route we were taking.

We were travelling too fast, too lightly, to be mistaken for tourists. We hit the trekker trail near Kharte, a village perched high above the river, and turned right for Lukla. Once again we felt unstoppable, but as we traversed the high mountainside, we gasped for breath and felt our legs grow wobbly.

Round about four o'clock, we asked a man how far it was to Lukla, but we didn't believe him when he indicated it was five hours. We knew better than that and set out to prove it. One and a half hours later we sighted the airfield and judged we'd be in Lukla before dark at 6 pm. It was just over there, just another down and up.

Confidently we took a short cut on a zigzag and then another that took us into sundown. It grew dark and the Lukla we knew was there had disappeared. Then suddenly we saw its lights. Our hearts sank. It was still over there. We'd blown it. We were stranded in the dark on the wrong mountain.

We decided to back-track – our first such move of the trip – down a spidery path in the dark. Cursing, we stumbled along, tripping on roots and rocks, until we found the right path. After almost fourteen hours non-stop and 11,000 feet of climbing, we finally arrived. Unbounded elation at reaching this milestone! By our reckoning, 272 miles from Darjeeling in ten days. We wanted to shout our achievement but no one was listening and the Mountain Travel representative was cool and unimpressed. He gave us our mail and directed us to a hotel. Here we ordered up a celebratory tea and we settled down to devour our post.

One letter was in Dad's handwriting marked 'First. Read this before all others.' It started 'Dear Boys, the news is sad . . .'

Our Mum, Beryl Crane, had died. She had died three days before we started out from Darjeeling. We had only known that she had been ill for some time.

Our father's immediate reaction was not to tell us because he feared we might give up the expedition. But by the next day and after a family discussion, it was obvious that we would have to be told. As it happened, the news failed to get to Darjeeling despite Steve Bonnist's efforts to contact us. Dad then wrote a long letter in which he made it clear that friends and relatives believed we should continue. He added the thought that 'Mum would have wished you to go on', and the hope that her death would spur us to greater efforts.

He was glad 'in his innermost heart' that we weren't told of our mother's death before we began. In retrospect, so were we. But at the time, the news came as a blow and, despite our father's attitude, the dilemma we faced was real: what was the right thing to do?

On the one hand, if we abandoned the expedition, we would let down so many people. This included Intermediate Technology, who'd supported us when we needed it most. We couldn't just give up even though we might have been excused if we did. For Adrian, who in a weaker moment had already contemplated injuring himself to end the run, our mum's death might have presented an honourable way out. Except that he didn't think like that.

We'd come such a long way, after all. We'd taken nearly thirty years to get this far. Surely there was no turning back? But could we go the whole way? That was another question.

We read Dad's letter again. It was perfectly clear. We had to carry on, at least for the time being. Apart from anything else, we owed it to him. When you analysed it, it was he who had guided us to the foot of Everest and our greatest challenge. Not only had he introduced us to the outdoors but he also fostered a spirit of adventure by not stifling our initiative or preventing us from taking risks.

8

At Lukla

THE NEWS OF Mum's death took a while to really sink in. Ados and I just sat there, stunned. Lost and confused. I wanted to cry but there were no tears. My eyes were dry.

My Mum was dead. We were hungry and worn out and covered in salt and grime. My hair was filthy and knotted. We tried filling our emptiness with food and drink as though it would somehow dull our senses. Or drown our feelings. I would never see her smile again, never feel her hug again. My Mum had died. It was as stark as that.

We ate yak meat and vegetables, fried rice, meat dumplings, fried Tibetan bread, chicken soup, pancakes. We had glass upon glass of chai and for afters a small bottle of rum and two bars of chocolate. Mum would have been delighted to see her boys eating so well. Then we had some coffee and finished the rum. And I sat down and wrote my diary.

I knew what Dad and the family felt about our going on but I wondered about Michèle. Did she think I ought to return? Or did she agree I should continue?

I wrote a full account of our day. How we'd set out from camp with the fourteen blokes of the First Cheshire. How warm the early sun was and how green and gentle the slopes were, like the Cotswolds of our childhood. How we said goodbye to the army climbers and 'rocketed onwards'. I described our first view of the Solo Khumbu valley – its wide stretch of well-kept terraces, the Sherpas' stone houses, the snowy peaks above us in the distance and far below the dusty trails the trekkers took . . . and how we got to Lukla. How 'we eat to avoid thinking'.

At 1 am I bedded down and at 3.30 I was still awake. My legs ached too much. My hips hurt on the hard boards. My brain wouldn't let me relax and, when eventually I slept, I had bad dreams. I was awake at six. And I bet every other trekker in Lukla was asleep, the lucky sods.

I'd say that Ados was much more affected by the news from home than I was. Piled on top of the physical trial he'd been through, it had shattered him. In his diary he couldn't bring himself to even mention Mum's death. Only: 'On receiving news we fill our minds and bodies with food. What else to do?' He did, however, write a letter to himself which described his sadness. Unlike me, he didn't want to expose his intimate thoughts but reading his customary understatement, you could see his sentiments between the lines: 'Today is another day and Dick acts normally but I think underneath he is very wrapped up, trying to work things out. I've written home and want to write a letter to Karen. I'm so glad that Mum knew her.'

We pushed on as per schedule in the late morning, having posted our family letters and pile of stuff to Kathmandu on the early plane. The route we were on was well-trodden. Probably about 10,000 tourists fly in for the eight-day trek each season. It would take us two days or so, up to Namche Bazar, on past the Thyangboche monastery, then Pangboche with Ama Dablam to our right, on to Pheriche and up to the Everest Base Camp. On paper it looks very flat, but it's hard to describe how extraordinarily steep this country is. Everything has been magnified to double the size: the mountains, their pinnacles glowing yellow in the early morning sunlight, are twice as high as you'd imagined, the river gorges twice as deep, and the prices twice as great.

This section of our traverse – the trip up to Everest Base Camp – was technically a diversion. We could legitimately head westward from Namche Bazar to Kathmandu. But it was an excursion into terrain so high and dramatic and famous that it was irresistible, simply as a sight to see. Another thing that had grown irresistible in our minds was the idea of a record-breaking rush from the Everest Base Camp to Kathmandu.

My diary, written the morning after hearing of Mum's death, was very positive. I noted that 'our optimistic schedules seem well and truly realistic' and, although the run we were anticipating was taking shape in our imaginations as a 'massive, dark, pulsating, wobbly blob of agony – 160 sweaty miles and "n" thousand feet of climbing, in a totally impossible three days', it was something we were mentally prepared to carry through.

'Beyond Kathmandu,' I added cautiously, 'nothing exists.'

By lunchtime we'd reached Namche Bazar, a famous name in the Everest story and the biggest village in Khumbu, at the junction of the Dudh Kosi and the Bhote Kosi. Since the arrival of the first European in the village in 1950, Namche has become an important administrative town without apparently losing its old character. It's got a school, police station, several open-fronted shops which stock the trekkers' treats – tinned stuff and souvenirs. Tatty little boards advertise 'restaurants' and 'hotels'. In Nepal, however, you sleep on the mat. In fact, here and elsewhere on the Himalayan trail, hotels are more often than not a total misnomer. Most of the ones we stayed in amounted only to floor space on the family hearth.

On the way to Namche, Ados picked up a tiny pebble from the path as a memorial stone for Mum. He wanted something he could hold on to; and he would carry it with him all the way.

I picked a flower. One of the little blue clusters which were scattered all over the grassy glades among the pines. I 'button-holed' the fragile thing on the top of my front pack so that I could see it. I knew it would wither and die but I'd picture it in bloom as I pictured my mother. Before, when I said something like, 'the thing about Mum is she's always there,' it meant she was an ever-present physical figure – at the door to welcome us or in the kitchen to feed us. Now I realised more exactly what ever-present meant: her memory would never leave my mind.

Around me, nature rose in soaring spires and I'd never seen a more uplifting

31

mountainscape. I felt my mother closer than ever before. And she would lighten my load.

Ados, I know, was also moved. 'What a wonderful place,' he wrote, 'to grieve for our mother.'

Most travellers are enthralled by the Khumbu scenery and travel writers compete to describe the 'stark grandeur', the 'stupendous view', the lovely scarlet, pink, white and yellow of rhododendron blossoms, the forests 'besprinkled with white magnolia flowers, heavily scented, fallen from the trees'.

On Day 11, we saw Mount Everest. Adrian wrote: 'Light and mountains fabulous. See Everest in clear skies. Should be the big moment of my year but . . .'

9

To the Foot of the Giant

AT SIX O'CLOCK on Day 11 we reached Thyangboche Monastery. Rebuilt after a fire in the thirties, it has a mediaeval look about it. Nearly fifty lamas live in a village community boxed in by white walls. They boast their monastery is 'the religious centre of the whole Sherpa-land'.

We spent the night in the travellers lodge with a number of trekkers and Austrian climbers heading for Ama Dablam. Ados was nourished by the company and in the morning he enjoyed 'a lovely visit to the monastery loo' with its view of Ama Dablam and Everest over Lhotse ridge.

Outside in the sun, I sat at the base of the main 'chorten' – the distinctive Buddhist monuments which characterise this area – and looked out over the upper Khumbu to Everest itself. Above me thin prayer flags, attached like sparse bunting to the chorten spire, fluttered their constant message to the winds: 'Om Mane Padme Hum'. It's a prayer heard all over this part of Tibetan Nepal and I suppose it is the Buddhist's Lord's Prayer and Creed rolled into one.

'Englishmen have told me,' says Tenzing in his book, 'that it sounds like "Money-penny-hum" repeated over and over, again and again. It is the sacred, mystical chant of Buddhism. What it literally means is "the jewel is in the lotus" but it also has many hidden and symbolic meanings which only the most learned lamas can understand . . .'

'Om mane padme hum . . . om mane padme hum . . .'

From Thyangboche we took our time up the valley to Pheriche. As impetuous as we were, we didn't want to be laid low with altitude sickness. Like a deep-sea diver who has to come up gradually to avoid the bends, we needed a slow ascent to allow our heads and lungs to adjust to less oxygen. Even so, we pushed it a bit and decided to stay overnight at 15,150 feet in the tiny stone hut at Dughla.

Our hosts were a deaf old man, his weather-beaten wife, and their young daughter who seemed to do all the house-work, busily feeding wispy bunches of heather into a ravenous fire. This was in the centre of the room and, unlike the fireplaces in the lower villages, this had a smoke hood and a chimney. A yak driver down from the Base Camp joined us and we all crowded round the fire in our thick duvets and big jackets.

I slept well, warm in my mountain equipment bag, but woke in the middle of the night for a gigantic pee brought on no doubt by the fact that we continued to drink masses of tea and weren't sweating it out. I crept outside. At two in the morning the world was absolutely still, the streams had frozen and the yaks stood solidified into fur stacks. The stars blinked and the moon put a sheen on the snow slopes.

The small squat hut in which Adrian, the yak driver and the family slept, crouched into the hillside, its roof edge serrated by icicles. It was an amazing atmosphere. I really was in a different world.

Back in my bag I lay awake, excited and apprehensive about our big run to Kathmandu. We had reached 'K-day'.

By nine o'clock in the morning of Day 13, Ados and I had reached Lobuche. We made our way along a narrow path between rocky crags, up over a stony moraine and frozen streams. We were now well and truly in the land of the big 'uns, eye-level it seemed with Ama Dablam and Pumori, but the Everest fortress was hidden by the walls that fronted it.

The trail then led us onto the flat expanse of Gorak Shep, the base camp for the 1952 Swiss expedition which nearly beat the British to the summit. Here there is a small lake, usually frozen, and several monuments reminding one of those who'd died on Everest. From this point the walk to Base Camp and back is estimated at six hours but we were aiming to cut that, and might have done except we ran into a problem: we got lost.

Because of shifting forces, the route up the Khumbu glacier is an ever-changing one and neither of us knew exactly where the Base Camp was. Nor is it a specific site. We therefore had no idea where the American expedition had pitched camp. Ados searched for a higher route and we became split up.

Where I went, I had to go quickly, jumping from boulder to boulder and relying on my speed and agility to save me if any of them rolled. It was easy at first but, dwarfed by the shapes around me, I imagined myself as a Lilliputian running over heaps of huge angular gravel. I was soon exhausted and had to stop for breath. Ados was nowhere in sight and I suddenly felt terribly lonely and vulnerable. The ice seracs were massive and dormant and the silence was alive!

Above me I could hear muffled rumblings and the crash of debris – deep distant roars playing bass to the high-pitched clink of falling rocks and ice. I clambered on, over what seemed to be a frozen lake with shark-tooth ridges running across it. The earth seemed to groan under the unwelcome weight of my feet. It creaked and heaved.

The only other time I've encountered terrain so rough was in the Galapagos Islands when I took gawping visitors over razor sharp lava flows. Here, at the foot of the giant, rocks and ice blocks five feet square and twenty feet high, were piled in tortured confusion. Any minute one might decide to crush me and I was terrified.

Looking back, I wouldn't have had it otherwise because part of the adventure game is to take you where you've never been before. To parts of yourself that you've never seen before. Now, with heart pumping, I struggled on alone.

I eventually spotted the flapping tents and low stone wind-shelters of the American Base Camp. As I staggered in with my tiny backpack and without Ados, I felt a bit of a twit. It's downright crazy arriving as I did, by myself, carrying no food and no spare clothes. And how was I to explain I was 'Running the Himalayas' with my brother, whom I'd lost! I needn't have worried. I caused exactly no stir on entering the encampment.

Two tall hunking Americans, one with a beard and the other with the proud title 'Doctor', were moving pebbles about. I said 'Hello' and nothing happened. I poked my head into the Sherpas' plastic-sheeted shelter and they smiled back at me, offered me tea and asked where my porters were. Revitalised by the tea, I made an assault on the icy cool of the Americans but they responded indifferently to my story. They did inform me that they were from 'Boulder Colorado, where all real climbers come from'. Then they let me write on a packing box in one of the tents to fill in my diary. It was then 1 pm and I thought that our run to Kathmandu would have to be postponed. I wondered where Ados was.

Before I left the camp I persuaded one of the Americans to sign a note saying that I had actually been there, but I had a problem trying to get a photo of this Base Camp visit because Ados had the camera. Eventually I persuaded them to take one picture of me, which they undertook to send me if I wrote to them in the summer. I shook their hands, put on my best pantomime smile and headed off towards Gorak Shep as quick as my little legs would carry me. I had to find Ados.

10

To the Top of Barf and Back

AS SMALL BOYS, we were not too keen on the great outdoors. Our father used to take us on outings to the Lake District fells where we tramped a bit, snowballed and tobogganed, all without much enthusiasm. Nor did we appreciate the dark and stormy night Dad made us climb Sty Head. We were both terrified and I remember my fear of being attacked by sheep.

I hated the hills in those days. And it must have been so obvious, that my father was afraid he'd frightened us off for good. As a result, he decided to let us find our own feet. This paid off after we moved to Seat Howe Villa, a house at Thornthwaite above Bassenthwaite Lake in Cumbria.

Situated on the slope of the hill, with a forest behind it, Seat Howe was a quarter of a mile from its neighbour and a few miles from Keswick where we went to the local grammar school. Each day we caught the bus and this was the vehicle for my first romance. I can joke about it now, but as Adrian says it was a 'touching two-year infatuation with the reflection of a girl in the front window of the bus'. In summer we canoed and paddled in the lake, and in winter we played hide-and-seek on the hill. It was here that the Bishop of Barf entered our lives.

A mere 1536 feet, Barf is a rugged pyramid with a 'hostile and aggressive character'. According to A. C. Wainwright, a noted lover of the Lakeland fells, its 'unrelenting steepness is allied to unstable runs of scree and outcrop [and] passers-by look up at Barf with no thought of climbing it'.

In 1782, however, the Bishop of Derry took a wager that he would mount it on his horse. He was en route to take up his post in Ireland and he broke his journey at The Swan with Two Necks (now The Swan). After looking too deep into the wine bottle, he bet fellow guests he could make it to the top. Halfway up, the horse stumbled, the Bishop tumbled and died.

Since then, the rocky pinnacle near the scene of his death has been known as 'The Bishop of Barf' and the publicans at The Swan have, by tradition, kept it whitewashed. Consequently, the Bishop can be seen for miles.

Looking back, we see the old Bishop as an unforgettable and influential character in our growing up. For the six years that our family lived in Seat Howe, he was there every day, overlooking the house.

As teenagers, we and our friends, the Hampson lads from The Swan, started racing up to the Bishop and back and also right to the top and back. We timed each other – 18½ minutes to the peak and six minutes down. The steepness that looked so impossible from the road was soon a piece of cake to us. To make it more interesting, we started scrambling up with rucksacks filled with rocks. This only made it slower.

These were the heady days, the carefree and happy part of our upbringing, full of adventures on the hills and play dens in the forests. Miles from town life, we had no interest in street gangs, discos, clothes, the other sex, smoking or drinking.

'It was much more exciting,' says Adrian, 'to climb a tree, blow up a bee hive or crash a car through the snow on Forestry Commission tracks.'

Motor cars became Adrian's obsession and for years he wanted to be a world champion racing driver – an ambition stirred by driving our oldest sister's bubble-car and a night spent in the forest watching the RAC Rally go through. The roar of each car, the blaze of headlights and sparks from flying stones was all thrilling stuff. So too was the dark and quiet and the anticipation which mounted before the next car. Then the cry would go up again: 'Car! Car!' and Ados' little heart would leap again.

In next to no time Ados had picked up a Triumph Herald from the local garage, and converted it into a bodiless charger. This was the first of many cars in which he careered around the Forestry tracks, pretending to be a rally driver and doing foolhardy things.

I didn't share this dare-devil interest or have the same mechanical aptitude. Nor, for that matter, did I take to winter climbing as quickly as my younger brother.

'Dick wasn't much of an outdoor adventure man in those days,' says Ados. 'He wore big black plastic spectacles and thought so much about all the inadequacies of his actions that he was usually too scared to give it a go. I think he only began to get a grip on himself and realise his capabilities when we went mountaineering in Scotland with Dad and Uncle Hol.'

Initially, I hated these trips too but I saw the invitation to join Uncle and Dad on their annual holiday ritual as an acknowledgement that I was no longer just a boy. In some respects it was a rite of passage, an initiation to manhood, and I resented the fact that Ados at only 15 should have been invited at the same time. This was an insult to my Big Brother status.

'I knew it bothered him,' says Adrian, 'but I was only too delighted, and frankly didn't know why he was so steamed up. Besides, I never ever queried or challenged his dominant role. Nor did I need to. Nor did I have the same need to get up Barf first. Or be fastest round the Forest track. But to Dick these things were important. He wasn't going to get beaten if he could help it, not by me or the snowy mountains.'

On the contrary, I became increasingly daring and competitive whether climbing, potholing or cycling.

Uncle Hol's winter expedition of 6–12 people travelled in Landrovers and caravans to the Scottish mountains for about ten days over the New Year. The idea was to get away from the crowds and comforts of home and town, to find the most remote mountains and try to climb them, preferably in the worst possible weather.

'For the first year or two we didn't do anything spectacular – just straightforward walks in the snow,' says Ados. 'But we quickly learned what failure was and we were pretty free with the word "impossible". That peak, we'd say, was "impossible to climb" or "it's impossible for anyone to go out in a blizzard like this" or "it's impossible to get there and back in that time". But as time went on we dropped "impossible" from our vocabulary. We would, for instance, go out in absolutely atrocious weather and come back twelve hours later in the same ferocious weather, soaked, numb, aching, exhausted, exhilarated, having climbed another "impossible" peak.'

What we younger generation of Cranes learned was that it was always worth attempting a challenge because 'it may just be possible'. We grew more confident and round the campfire with our brother Christopher, cousin Nick and our mate Klon, we started talking about challenges beyond the Highlands. We wanted to do something that would test our survival skills to the utmost, to discover how far we could stretch ourselves, before it was too late.

Travel widened our horizon. At the age of sixteen, Ados and I journeyed around East Africa. Adrian also went cycling in France and Switzerland and, after collecting my geology degree at Durham University, I sped to the South Pacific and the Galapagos, where I was a tourist guide for a year. I reckon this was the most influential year in my education. I developed an enquiring mind, at last questioning what was going on in the world. And I discovered women!

I followed my Galapagos year by hiking and hitching around the Andes in South America, travelling alone in Ecuador, Peru and Bolivia, through coastal desert and Amazonian jungle, along the ancient Inca trail to Machu Picchu. I also climbed Cotopaxi, which at 19,354 feet is the world's highest volcano.

Then I thumbed my way across the United States from Florida to California and back east to New York. In England I decided, for a career's sake, to add a doctorate to my name. I hooked a research offer from Oxford but chose instead to go to Reading University. At the age of 25, I still retained some of my old naivety. Unbelievably, I had no idea that an Oxbridge degree carried greater weight than others.

My father's puritannical philosophy about education is that 'you have to submit yourself to a discipline and conquer it'. I'm sure this is how I live and I suppose it explains much about me. For four years I slogged at a thesis titled 'A Computer Model for the Architecture of Avulsion-Related Alluvial Suites'. I worked all hours, for long periods averaging only five or six hours sleep a night.

But it wasn't all work. I met Michèle and spent every minute I could with her. When she went off to Grenoble in 1981 to teach for a year, I became a recluse, living in a little room at Whitley Park Farm in Reading. I went from my desk on one side of my room to my bed on the other. Student poor, I ate little, experimenting with no-meat diets, no-fat diets, no-salt diets and no-sugar diets. For days on end, I ate only dry toast and boiled vegetables. I can now confirm it isn't good for you!

All this – the anxiety and stubborn effort in my thesis, which was running overtime, and my spartan existence – were, in retrospect, good preparation for a life of deprivation and punishment. But if this wasn't enough, I further punished my system by taking to my bicycle and making forty to eighty mile training rides on my own.

In May 1982 I entered my first marathon run, the Stoke 'Around the Towns', and my time was a very modest four hours forty-five minutes, very nearly the same time I took to do a hundred miles on bicycle. In other bike time trials, I did twenty-five miles in one hour six minutes and 225 miles in twelve hours. These weren't records, but proof that I could cycle seriously if need be, especially in endurance events.

In August 1982 I was elected to membership of the Nosey Ferret Racing Team. This dynamic group of enthusiasts captured the world speed record for human-powered two-wheeled vehicles and I piloted one of their experimental three-wheelers. In the international human-powered vehicle championship I came eighth out of forty at Brands Hatch, and averaged 37.2 mph in the flying quarter-mile.

Come October and the Cumbria Marathon, I knocked nearly two hours off my first time, finishing in two hours fifty four minutes.

I ran it under three hours because it was going to be the last serious athletic thing that I would ever do. I put everything into it and couldn't bend my legs enough to climb the stairs for two days afterwards. The whole idea was to settle down into my career and share my time with Michèle.

But Ados, of course, had other ideas.

Like me, Adrian did a geology degree at Durham and celebrated his BSc (Hons) with a trip to Morocco and the northern reaches of the Sahara. He then went off and did an MSc in Management Science at Imperial College in London. On finishing, job opportunities opened before him. One contract took him to Riyadh in Saudi Arabia where he took to motor cycling in the desert.

In 1980 he transferred to Taif, also in Saudi Arabia, where he worked and walked, climbed mountains, dived into the Red Sea and met Karen Sue Hatfield of Modesto, California. Smitten, he roared back to Britain from Saudi on his motorbike and flew to the USA where he found his love and well-paid work as a computer consultant in Silicon Valley, California. In November 1981 he ran the San Francisco Marathon – his first ever. He also got back into rally driving, teaming up with Topi Hynynen, for the US National Rally championships and other events including the East of Indio (California) Rally which they won. But he no longer had the same passion for the sport. His heart was set on doing something extraordinary.

A few years back, he and our younger brother Christopher (who, incidentally, has climbed all 216 peaks in the Lake District) had done The Three Peaks – a non-stop race by car, in the middle of winter, to climb Ben Nevis, Scafell Pike and Snowdon, the highest peaks in Scotland, England and Wales. Their time, from the start (dipping their fingers in the sea near Ben Nevis) to the finish (dipping their fingers in the sea at Carnarvon) was just under fifteen hours.

Not to be outdone, cousin Nick and I then did the trial by bicycle – 460 miles up and down in forty-two hours twenty minutes, including twelve hours on the mountains. And if it hadn't been for blizzard conditions on Snowdon, we might have broken the record.

It was from the Three Peaks trial that Ados had come up with the whopper: the Seven Peaks: climb to the top of the highest mountain on every continent. Not exactly easy since it obviously includes a few minor problems like Mount Everest! No one has ever done it but to make it harder Ados proposed to do it all in one year – Everest in Asia, the Cartstenz Pyramids in Australasia, Elbruz in Russia,

Mount McKinley in North America, Aconcagua in South America, Kilimanjaro in Africa and the Vinson Massif in Antarctica.

It was an incredible idea and Ados even had a batch of letter heads printed to get things going. But he had no takers.

Not surprisingly, Everest as a challenge remained near the top of his list. But on Day 13 in the Himalayas, he was running away from it.

11

The Race for Kathmandu

Day 13

Adrian: I left my high point over Everest Base Camp at 1.15 pm and moved very slowly down a ridge, watching for signs of Dick among the cluster of tents that was below me. I decided the best thing was to go back to Gorak Shep and wait for him. A couple of Japanese who had also had difficulty finding Base Camp signed my log 'close to EBC' as we sipped tea at Gorak Shep.

Richard: It took me just over two hours to get down from EBC to Gorak Shep and at 4.15 I was prepared to call it a day. I'd burnt up many hours worth of adrenalin in my frightening scramble and had an altitude headache. The Americans had angered me and I was despondent until Ados introduced me to the 'Yeti man', or more correctly, William B. Grant. A fascinating guy, he wanders the High Himalayas carrying a golf putter and looking for evidence of Yetis – the abominable snowmen. I would have loved to have spoken longer with him but Ados was impatient to get going and moved me into jogging gear, saying: 'Come on, it's downhill now to Kathmandu and a rest!' I went along, sloppily at first, but warmed up as we descended, following the porter trail and dodging the piles of yak shit. The late sun lit Pumori, Taweche and Ama Dablam in front of us. Everest, in the clouds, was behind us – another name to tick off.

Adrian: Ran down this big country till darkness – nearly three hours for ten miles and about 5000 feet of descent – then tramped into Pangboche for one of our uninvited ethnic nights. Both of us absolutely knackered but altitude headaches have faded. Occurred to me that I'd reached a new personal altitude record today. At least 18,500 feet, maybe 19,000. But Dick's been higher . . . 19,354 feet up Cotopaxi. I'd like to come back and dash all the way to the top: from a finger in the sea to a hand on the Chinese maypole at the summit. That hasn't been done before.

Friday 1st April: Day 14

Richard: At 5.30 am we took a swig of water, walked for a quarter of an hour to loosen up, then ran in crystal clear air. We are really on our way now; once more exhilarated by the mountainscape and our challenge. Ados has calculated it can be done in three days! As we approached Thyangboche the sun sparkled on the

41

monastery's golden spire. We paused for tea and a last glance back at Everest and rose once more to slither 1500 feet to the river, heading for a big breakfast at PK's hotel in Namche Bazar and then on to Lukla.

Adrian: My stomach feels a bit uneasy. I think it's trying to tell me something.

Richard: For the next 145 miles or so to Kathmandu we are below the snow line, back among the trees, the flowers, the people and the more humid warmth of the lower hills. It means we can safely jettison our high-altitude, heavyweight gear and reduce our already shrunken packs to a super-spartan level.

'We've left our balaclavas on a 'mani' wall to be picked up by the first passer-by, swopped our gloves for smiles with a few villagers and given our thermal underwear to the Cheshire 'Acorns' whom we ran into again, by chance, just south of Namche. They passed them on to their porters. We've cut off the legs of our long cotton trousers to make short shorts, and ditched our altitude sickness pills. So our packs are now down to seven pounds and we're positively light-hearted.

Adrian: At Lukla we lunched at the Holiday Inn and wrapped up our paper work. Up-dated our diaries and parcelled up our Gore-Tex weatherwear with letters and films for home.

Richard: I spared a thought for my shoes and wrote a letter to Tony Ward, our New Balance contact, telling him I've road-tested them over 300 miles, some of it on the roughest terrain imaginable. The soles have hardly worn but I've cut the sides on the glacier rocks, which isn't surprising since my crawling, clawing and clambering over the same moraine also wore out the fingers of my gloves!

Adrian: Out of Lukla, would you believe, we took the wrong path again and paid for it on a horrible piece of trail – sharp, steep, narrow and treacherous above the Dudh Kosi. Getting it wrong always depresses me. This was compounded by the realisation that our valuable films and diaries have been packed with gear that might be stolen.

Richard: I couldn't believe our stupidity! Our record of the past four days could be destroyed by one unscrupulous Nepali who fancied some expensive second-hand gear. All I had to do was post the films and papers under separate cover, but no! We cursed like mad but it didn't help and I think I was more depressed than Ados. All I could manage was to slog on behind him. And what a slog! We were on the old track to Jubing, having decided against the higher, straightforward, new road which is the Swiss contribution to the country's infrastructure. Zig and zag, slip and slide, up the crag and down the gorge – we knew it was going to be tough but we didn't anticipate such a tortuous haul.

Adrian: What a day for April Fools! Had a water stop and while trying to wash our prized water-'bottle' in a lively stream the lid leapt out of my hand and before we could snatch it back, went skiing off in the direction of the plains of India. So we parted company with our container as well. Now my calves are tight. Real achers. And my nose is sunburnt.

Richard: There's no jubilation in Jubing. I hated every step of the way and all I want is to arrive in Kathmandu and find our films and letters safe.

We're still east of the Dudh Kosi and only tomorrow will we start due west for Lamosangu, cutting right across the grain of this ridge-lined country. We've totally blown any hope of a three-day triumph! We've also been told that some chap by the name of Longacre claims to have done KTM to EBC in two and a half days. Although people who know him discount his claim and say he used local transport, the thought of anyone beating our attempt is irritating. We just have to believe in the evidence we've been given that we're still out on our own.

Adrian: There are eight travellers in this darkroom all waiting for dahl bhaat; the local staple of rice and lentil sauce. We've climbed in beside the only light, a smoky petrol flame, to write our diaries.

Day 15

Richard: Another 5.30 start and on the other side of the Dudh Kosi we must climb 5000 feet to a 9800-foot pass. In the rising sun we moved past Sherpa farmsteads and their terraces, bright green with young wheat shoots. At 8000 feet we entered a fir and rhododendron forest. The exotic bushes we know from home are, like other natural phenomena in this part of the world, more than we'd imagined. Here they're large trees with gnarled moss-covered trunks, and festooned with creepers. Emerging from the rhododendrons we came across the isolated Trakshinda Gompa. Reputed to be a superb example of Sherpa monastic architecture, it was disappointing. I was expecting something more splendid and bigger, more impressive Buddha statues, but the interior is rather worn out and dusty, and the Buddhas crude. I'm glad, however, that we went in.

Adrian: I could do without the ethnic diversions but Dick won't close down his sightseeing department. I am impatient with the irritations of this section and saffron-robed monks, for all their tolerance, do nothing for mine. At Junbesi, a lovely lady served us the very best noodle soup and apple pancake but her service was so slow, we lambasted her. I feel so guilty!

Richard: That very large bowl of noodle soup with a mix of beans and veg was the best I've ever had but we buried it in biscuits and oatflakes, then ran it into our bowels, up a climb of 2500 feet to Lamjura Bhanyang, an 11,350-foot pass. At Kenja, we bought a torch and batteries for forty rupees (£2) and, thus armed, ignored the temptation to stop at dusk. We brushed off the jokes shouted at us by porters who, wise enough to call it a day, were resting. On the narrow path, porters are a bind. Bent under their loads they don't see us until we're right on top of them. Then they stop and turn and block the path, making it difficult for whichever of us is following. It's like an Atari video-game of 'Dodging the Nepalis'.

Adrian: We followed our torchlight into Chyangma, found a good hotel, good food and had a good sing-song. I felt rested but thought of Kathmandu and the question of whether or not we carry on. Right then I was prepared to quit after a final rush. We were thinking of running all the way non-stop. Tomorrow to Kirantichap and then umpteen miles through the night. It didn't thrill me. Dick also irritated me with his enthusiasm. I bet his diaries are full of words like 'I'm exhausted – brilliant!' and 'another wonderful climb.' He also went on about the locals not eating their potato peels with all those extra vitamins and the roughage content. What with cyclists pedalling incorrectly and porters not eating the right stuff, Dick thinks he could teach the people of this sub-continent a thing or two.

Day 16

Richard: One and a half glasses of rakshi last night sent me to sleep drunk. So I was slightly hungover when we got up and generally a bit pained. My right knee hurt and it was an effort creaking to the village tap where I splashed my face and slipped in my contact lenses. I take them out each night, wrapping them in a tiny piece of cloth.

So far, we've been lucky because we've chanced our arms and legs a number of times, skipping and dancing on some rocky descents. If we broke anything we're nowhere near National Health.

We were set upon by the locals last night which explains the rakshi. Four Nepalis wandered in apparently in search of amusement. They ignored the fact that we were head down over our diaries and accosted us with all the usual demands: 'Where you going?', 'What is your country of origin?', 'Give me pen', 'Give me book', and 'Where you going?' again.

Eventually we capitulated and, what-the-hell, joined their drinking. It didn't take much for the singing to break out. We sang our French and English songs and they knocked off a few of their own. Fun stuff but we got to bed late at 10 pm and were paying the price.

I'm actually pissed off with the people in this part of the world. I'm talking about around Namdu where the attitude of the locals struck me as quite unpleasant. Unlike the Tibetan Sherpas with their round faced, big-eyed, smiling personalities, these Hindu people are short on charm. It seems the nearer we get to Kathmandu, the more abrasive and unfriendly the people are. They're sloppy and messy and have no work ethic.

Adrian: We reached Mynah Pokhri, the furthest that four-wheel drive vehicles can penetrate from Kathmandu, at about one o'clock. It's the end of the trekking trail and we had covered the seventy-five miles or so from EBC in almost exactly seventy-two hours. Three days! The distance includes climbs totalling 29,000 feet, the height of Everest. Kathmandu is, by our guesstimate, another ninety miles further on. We can do it tomorrow if we plough on through the night.

Richard: I was into the mindless churning of the miles. At the roadhead village of Kirantichap we were still going great guns and by the time we climbed to the larger town of Charikot we decided to go all the way.

At eight o'clock night had fallen. But we had two new torches. The trail wound uphill. Dogs barked at us. We donned our down jackets as we trudged upwards. We traipsed a cold, windy ridge at 10,000 feet in the moonlight. We went for hours, but each minute added to the aches and pains, which were minimal up to now. They sent messages to our brains, telling us to stop. But we were numbed with weariness and didn't heed them. We'd got to keep going because we said we would. Eventually our steps, already heavy, faltered. And we were practically sleep-walking. Ados, in fact, veered off the trail, stumbling into a bush. Enough is enough.

So we climbed a few feet above the trail and spread our sleeping bags on a terrace. Two am. We held the semi-recumbent position for one whole minute in order to enjoy not standing on our legs then were swept into deep sleep.

Day 17

Adrian: Awoke as the sun got up and about at 5 am. It took only moments to gather our goods and stumble back on to the trail. We stopped at the first crummy teashack we came to, boiled a couple of eggs because its Easter Monday, and sold our torches for half-price. They're too heavy to carry.

We must have done about twenty miles in the night, which means we started out this morning (near Murla) about eighteen miles from Lamosangu and sixty odd miles from Kathmandu. The trail descends and we followed it to the Sun Kosi valley, only 2000 feet above sea level and too many degrees above hot for me. In Lamosangu by 10 am. Only fifty miles to go. But the way I was feeling, too far for me.

Richard: 10.30 hours, Lamosangu on the Sun Kosi. Too tired to write anything.

Adrian: Such an endless road. Gave messages to a couple of motor-cyclists to take to Kathmandu. They were a tonic for us. Heat really intense. Drank continuously and poured water over my head at every opportunity. Terrible tea stop at 3 o'clock. Made me really feel ill.

Richard: 1700 hours. Morale rose as the distance became less. Forty miles – the distance we ran from Reading to London for breakfast TV; thirty miles – the distance from Keswick to Carlisle; soon it'll be twenty-six and a bit – a mere marathon distance.

Adrian: Dick still believed we could do another thirty miles or so without stopping. He didn't realise how painful my feet were or how battered I felt. I couldn't think straight. I just wanted to stop, but he dragged me on until five-ish. We stopped and he pushed tea and curried beans in front of me. He expected me to recover. I felt dreadful.

Richard: I ate my curried beans and drank gallons of tea to rehydrate. Ados had dropped like a sack of manure beside me and was only interested in sipping his tea. I told him things would be easier in the cool of the night and that his tea would revive him. That would make Kathmandu that night. I urged him on – to make one last big effort. He didn't argue and at six we set out again.

My feet and legs had been protesting their punishment for some time, but now each step was a jolt. Ados didn't say a word, but the sound of his effort was plain. We struggled for a mile or so, then Ados veered to the side of the road and vomited. He sank to his knees and was sick again. Only then did I admit defeat. We crawled back to a village we'd passed for a place to sleep. I thought, 'We're beaten, what a couple of failures we are!'

It was at this point that we ground to a halt. Morale, despite my afternoon optimism, hadn't risen enough to overtake fatigue and Adrian's sudden deterioration. He had had enough. It was clear to me that an accumulation of both physical and mental factors accounted for it. But I was convinced that, more than anything, the hellish heat that day had shot my brother's defences, that he'd been hit by sunstroke or heat exhaustion.

Our diaries until now had been noticeably low key on aches and pains. Certainly there were exclamations of weariness but for much of the time mine (not surprisingly) was full of how strong we were. But when we approached and crossed the threshold of our endurance, I suddenly realised how much I had been weakened. My feet were a mass of blisters; my left heel was bruised; my Achilles tendon and right knee threatened to give. On top of that, my stomach wasn't a hundred per cent – it wasn't even 50 per cent! So I needed to pull-up as well.

The following morning I got Adrian going again, who I think was able to respond only because the end really was just down the road. Nevertheless, he complained bitterly about how senseless it was to drive ourselves so hard, and at one of our stops, he wrote:

'Not another day. I just can't stand this. What is the point? What else can be proven except my insanity?'

He also asked why he had to *walk* into Kathmandu. One answer was because I was *making* him walk. Another was because he hadn't got where he was by giving up! As usual he didn't wax lyrical about the whys and wherefores of our situation.

Adrian: I didn't have to. Dick would do all that. He always had his sawn-off pencil out at moments like this when things looked dramatic or in need of analysis. When he wrote 'We've properly exhausted ourselves now', the satisfaction in the statement is implicit – he wouldn't have had it otherwise.

Richard: Of course, we had set out to stretch ourselves to the limit and in that we had now succeeded. One of the major objectives of the expedition was for us to try our damnedest – and go down fighting. Anything less than that and we could really say we'd failed. 'Running the Himalayas' had to be excruciatingly tough if it were to have any value. Now, almost there, we'd reached the most testing, crucial point – just the time for an objective assessment. The way I reasoned it, I had to step outside the problems in order to analyse our situation, for I was both guinea pig and scientific investigator.

Day 18

Richard: We've staggered on and done quite well so far, with seventeen kilometres to get to Dhulikhel and the signs say only thirty kilometres after that. Less than twenty miles. But we've properly exhausted ourselves now. Ados can't cope and my system isn't in good working condition.

We're now eighteen days from Darjeeling and it's possible that our breakdown has resulted from the accumulative effect of sustained activity. But I doubt this, since we felt so good at Lukla and all the way to Jiri. Our bodies failed because we started our all-out dash about a hundred miles from Kathmandu and the demand was too great. We just couldn't keep it up.

When we started we set no realistic time targets. Even the one hundred-day target for the entire traverse, our suggested arrival at Lukla on Day 10 and at Kathmandu on Day 17 were all guesswork. They were simply based on our experience in the Scottish hills and measurements on a large-scale map. They were produced because the media needed dates in advance. We ourselves gave them little substance. We saw the route as two sections: the first was the distance to the next town or the next junction in the trail, and the second section was all the remainder. We aimed for one target at a time.

We were surprised by the accuracy of our guesses as to when we would reach Lukla and Everest Base Camp. Then when we started the run down, we had hit three, four, five targets each day. The timing looked good. We grew over-optimistic and thought that our bodies were tougher than they were. I didn't fully realise the damage we were doing. We had exhausted our carbohydrate supply and were burning up our muscle protein.

But our big mistake was to push ourselves on after Charikot into the night. In fact, had we rested well the night before last, we'd have been in Kathmandu practically a day earlier. As it was, we failed to get there in four and a half days. And we were thinking of giving up altogether.

Adrian: The Dhulikhel Lodge where we rested was an oasis. It was cool and clean and I could have lain there all day. We planned to stop for an hour, which stretched into two 'as we (according to Dick) psyched ourselves up for the final push'. He actually got engrossed in his diary and, typically, was doing his homework preparation for our arrival in Kathmandu. My long sleep and this rest had restored some of my strength but I can't agree with Dick when he says things like: 'Refreshed, we set out anew with teeth clenched and fists tight, determined to grin and bear this final day and walk with heads held high'. I didn't have that sort of energy.

What provided the extra spurt came from meeting Margaret Percy, the BBC Radio Four reporter, and Gary Whitby, the laughing cavalier from Intermediate Technology. Our morale rocketed and Margaret's walk into town with us was, as I wrote that night, 'help beyond belief'. But I was still ready to quit.

Richard: We'd been trudging along counting every step and praying for the next mile-stone, but our friends' arrival on the scene had such an effect that the next ten miles went by almost without our noticing. The last eight miles, however, were long and hard again and, without support, would have been a nightmare.

We strode (sort of) into Durbar Square in the centre of Kathmandu at 4.30. Here we were welcomed by Lisa van Gruisen and a group of photographers. We were shaken by the hand, patted on the back, pressed to have tea and coffee, plied with questions and, before we knew it, ushered into a press conference at the Tiger Tops Mountain Travel Office.

Our relief at making it changed to a certain elation with all the attention. Obviously others didn't see us as failures. After all, we had established a record – from Everest Base Camp to Kathmandu on foot all the way in five days, two and a half hours. We had proved ourselves!

At the press conference, Ados did his party piece. He fell asleep!

12

Catching Up

IN KATHMANDU and booked in at the Malla Hotel, one of the poshest in town, we took stock. I looked in the mirror and was rather delighted by what I saw. I looked knackered and filthy. We *were* knackered and filthy.

'We've done Steve and IT proud,' I remarked. 'We've made it look like we're putting some effort into the trek!'

The effort, in turn, had taken its toll and by the following day, Day 19, I was suffering a reaction. I felt 'absolutely grotty' but we had to stay on our toes to cope with the consequences of our achievement. That meant handling correspondence, press calls, trunk calls to England and a round of social activities.

The most important thing we had to do was decide whether or not we should go on. Family enthusiasm, more support from Steve Bonnist, and a good press encouraged us to continue.

Ados was thinking of me: 'I didn't want to quit and let Dick down. Whatever he might say, it wasn't feasible for one to go it alone. By then we'd sussed that out – the day-to-day stuff, the route finding, forcing yourself to go on and on – it would have been an impossible strain. And if there were an accident or illness, there would be no back-up, no crutch for the guy to lean on. I mean, neither of us was on a suicide run.

'My pulling out would have solved my problems: I would have taken on a big challenge and failed. But, unfortunately, that would have left Dick further out on a limb. He'd still be needing that big expedition to prove himself because he'd been forced to stop on this one through no fault of his own. Yes, he could have tried it, a certain kind of solo traverse is possible, but the guy who tried it at our pace, well, he'd be my definition of a "nutter".'

The only other consideration was whether we should set off next day as planned or wait a bit till we recuperated. We decided that the sooner we got back on the road, the better, but the need to organise ourselves was the decider.

Three nights in Kathmandu were more than we'd scheduled but arriving as celebrities meant we had to devote so much time to the media and social obligations. The stay should have been restful, but it wasn't. We hadn't caught up on our sleep, we wrote no less than 132 post cards and eight letters; we met and talked to many people; sorted our equipment, medicines, maps, papers and films and ate far too much for tender digestive systems.

On our last night we worked so late – sewing and snipping until about two in the morning – that we only got four hours sleep. We actually looked forward to getting back to the hills, to early nights and eight hours of sleep, away from all our 'office work', the necessity to meet so-and-so and talk to whatsisname. But as soon as we started again, it all seemed too much.

We left Kathmandu on the morning of Day 21, one day behind schedule. Once again it was fun to be the centre of attention and, once again, as in Darjeeling, we acted blasé about the trials up ahead, our stamina and fitness. The difference, however, was that in Darjeeling we had no real expectation of succeeding. Now we had reputations to live up to!

We waved goodbye to our Mountain Travel friends and the others who had gathered to see us off. We ran round the square and, the moment we were out of sight, began to walk. Our target was Trisuli Bazar, about thirty miles away.

There was nothing in the least romantic about Kathmandu now. It was hot and dusty and irritating work making our way through the streets that were crowded with buses, bikes, rickshaws, barrow pushers, dossers, dogs and cows. Tiny children squatted in puddles, playing 'houses' with mud, stones and rotten fruits. Older children pestered us with their 'Hellos' and 'Bye-byes'. No one seemed to look where they were going. One man turned blindly in front of me and our collision knocked him into the gutter where he lay, looking aghast.

Out along the asphalt streets, through the squalid suburban sprawl, and eventually out of town. It would be much better, I thought, when we'd climbed from the Kathmandu valley. But my body didn't much fancy the idea.

We stopped for what, a few days ago we relished as a welcome cup of chai – hot, sweet, milky tea. But it was disgusting. We tried another place across the road – it was just as awful. There were flies crawling all over the potato curry and the peeled, boiled eggs on a shelf. We paid for the tea and left the full cups to fester on the bench. How the hell could we survive on this sort of fare? For another 2000 miles?

One by one, aches and doubts returned to plague us. Dormant blisters came alive. Ados said his legs were hurting. I said my head ached. Worst of all, the sun and heat had renewed their assault and Ados was starting to wilt badly again. At three o'clock, after five hours, we made the rim of the Kathmandu Valley. I flashed a V-sign at the city and turned for the Trisuli River valley. We realised that another small segment of our journey was out of the way. We had chalked up our first victory over the rest of the route!

The long mountain spur led us down a 2000 foot descent, through dusty terraces to a lovely wet valley where rice planting was in full swing. Young boys and girls were fashioning delicate aqueducts and waterworks out of lumps of wood and rounded stones and packing the channels with clods of earth. Men with sticks in their hands whistled and grunted at ponderous grey buffaloes dragging their ploughs through the quagmire. We stopped to enjoy the benefits of a water well in the middle of a cluster of white-washed houses with thatched roofs. Bundles of corn were suspended under the eaves and wooden sickles and scythes hung from crooked beams. Mediaeval England on a summer's day was probably just as beautiful and equally unhurried. We wandered on across stepping stones, then tiptoed along the narrow walkways which thread the paddies. In the splashing of the streams and the gentleness of the greenery, we lost track of time and found ourselves, at dusk, on the wrong side of a very wide river.

We waded across it and went on, splashing through paddy fields in the dark. A little village gave us dahl bhaat and a crowd of men and boys gathered to watch us eat. Afterwards we rolled our sleeping bags out on reed mats and lay down beside two very young children. Goats were tethered in the next room and big clay storage jars stood against the wall. With blisters, headaches, stomach problems and weariness, we were asleep before the onlookers crept away.

We ought to have taken it easier, but we had set ourselves an ambitious target for that day and once again had pushed ourselves and failed to reach it. What's more, we were still a good walk short of Trisuli Bazar.

We dallied the next morning, delaying the agony of getting started. The distance across the Himalayas seemed so huge that hurrying now would make no difference. There was no wind and the heat was oppressive. A stagnant haze filled the sunless sky. The road was dry and dusty. We went very slowly, only sprinting when we had to make for the bushes to beat our racing bowels.

My diary records that 'drive, energy and inspiration have completely failed me', and that my left heel blisters 'hurt like buggery'. But I laughed when Ados tried on his revamped trousers. We'd got to Trisuli and stopped in a crummy looking chai house where I deposited my brother. He sat around in his underpants drinking Fanta Orange while I went off with his long trousers to find a tailor. An hour later I returned, sporting new shorts, and Ados came out from behind his table to put his on. Their diagonal cut was just what he'd ordered – short at the back to allow for easy leg movement and long in the front to protect his knees from the sun. He stood there unshaven and bleary-eyed, on rubbery legs. A helpless specimen. Hardly able to raise a smile.

'What a pair of scarecrows!' I said. 'We look as though we couldn't run across a field let alone along these bloody mountains.'

'You're beginning to notice,' said Ados rather stiffly. Then he added: 'I think we should have an early night.'

'Anything you say, brother,' I agreed. And it was only two o'clock!

Three miles the other side of Trisuli Bazar we came upon a little clump of thatched houses tucked away among the trees. A clear stream flowed past a little slate walkway. We sat on a stone beneath a large shady tree and decided to stay the night. Several children stopped their games to stare at us. When an elderly man came out of one of the houses to inspect us, we tapped our stomachs.

'Khanna dinus?' we asked. 'Will you give us food?'

He nodded and beckoned us to follow him. Rucksacks off our backs, weight off our feet, we relaxed at last on the clay floor of the patio outside his house. We looked out across a few rough cattle shelters thatched with leaves and over the cobbly river and the bright green squishy paddy fields it watered, to the hillside beyond. Grey brown terraces climbed up 1000 feet to another group of houses and then on into the trees above. Our village had banana trees, a papaya, a few green mango trees and the customary large tree under which we'd been sitting. A few chickens, one sleepy dog and a handful of people wandered about.

Three or four old men appeared to be living in one house with about the same number of women whose ages ranged, at a guess, from twenty to eighty. In addition, there were six little boys and five toddlers. A couple of straw mats were brought for us to sit on and we settled down to a peaceful evening trying to unwind, forget the traverse, forget the mountains and forget the world beyond this haven we had found.

I rose to the new day with a feeling of urgency. It was Day 23 of our run. I jumped out of my bag, eager to get moving, but Ados was still asleep and I had to drag him up. Then drag him along behind me. It wasn't long before I was thinking that if things did not improve soon we might have to think about splitting up and I would go on alone. We were dropping further and further behind schedule whenever Ados insisted on stopping for a rest. I argued that we should keep going steadily and our illnesses would clear themselves. Ados was equally adamant that we should stop and recuperate.

'I feel terrible,' he said to his diary. 'Legs like lead and jelly. Stomach like a massive gallstone. Whatever Dick says about the power of the mind, a few days rest is needed to cure this. He seems to think that we can continue pushing ourselves and we will recover regardless. I know I cannot give up till Dick is prepared to and he will just never agree!'

That evening we were encamped on a small verandah near the Ankhu Khola river. It had started raining and big blobs spattered around us. Once more we were depressed.

'There's no real reason for us to stop,' I said to Ados.

'What about our feet, our stomachs? We're just becoming more and more run down.'

'Yeah, but these things must get better.'

'Not unless we stop . . .'

'Look! We've been going slower and slower and we can go on slowly for a bit more. But there's no reason to stop.'

'That's not going to reduce our problems. We'll probably add to them; make them worse. Then we really would have to pack up.'

'While they're not terminal we can always go another step.'

'That's what you think!'

Apart from whether we could hold up or not, we also differed on the best way of making progress and how fast we should go. Ados preferred to sleep long and have long food stops but travel fast in between. I thought we should get up earlier to travel in the cool hours and then just keep going, only eating quickly wherever possible on the way. By 'travelling fast', Ados really meant not stopping for things he regarded as a waste of time and energy, like the people and their culture. He had his blinkers on.

I had a natural interest in things around me and also knew IT would be interested. Consequently, I tried to learn about farming techniques, the sort of fireplaces people had and the fuel they burned. I was also invariably prepared to stop and have a look at some of the machinery, such as the grain mills, that we came across and explore the villages we stopped in. Of course, the worse Ados felt, the less he was inclined to

Ados leads Dick along a high trail above the oasis of Muktinath near the Annapurna Himal. Note the little back packs, small front packs, running shoes and balaclavas used as sun shades. *Day 34.*

Two porters on the main trail we followed through paddy fields in Nepalese foothills.

Ados in a three-sided tunnel cut by Nepalese porters into the valley walls of the Kali
Gandhaki which cuts the deepest gorge in the world between the two 8,000 m peaks of
Annapurna and Dhaulagiri. *Day 35.*

Villagers near Taka (Dhorpatan) stare at Ados. *Day 39.*

Sharing a welcome bathe at Tatopani hot springs. *Day 36*

Smoke and wood at Taka. *Day 39.*

Ados leads out over the paddy fields of Nepal.

Dick (*left*), Ados (*centre*), with umbrellas to shade themselves in the 110° F heat of Nepalese plains near Indian border. *Day 49.*

Dick puts his hands together for the traditional 'Namaste' greeting to chai house owner and locals in the Garwhal Indian foothills. *Day 59.*

A Zanskari woman proudly displays her turquoise head-dress which reflects her family's wealth. *Day 73-78.*

Young Tibetan nomad collecting yak dung at 13,000 ft to dry for fuel.

tolerate such diversions. He just wanted to go from one point to the next as quickly as he could get there. The problem was that our rest stops were becoming more frequent and I feared we would succumb to the temptation of following each half hour of trek with an hour's tea break. We were, in fact, reaching a crisis.

The following day found us in a particularly pleasant and fertile stretch of country and I wanted to take photographs. Ados, however, wasn't in the mood for that sort of dawdling and pressed on, leaving me behind with the camera. I knew I could catch him up and once more contemplated going on alone. But when I found him two hours along the trail, outside a little village shop, he had collapsed again, overcome by diarrhoea and vomiting.

'This went on,' Ados wrote, 'for four hours until I'd nothing left to give. Dick shifted us from the public glare of the shop to a slightly less crowded farmhouse where I spent the rest of the day on my back. At one point he returned from a look around the village with a perfect papaya. It looked so juicy and delicious that I tried a piece the size of a postage stamp – and was promptly sick.'

I didn't realise just how ill Ados was until I arrived at Sallentar and found him laid out. Up till then I'm afraid I thought his complaints were little more than an excuse for a break. I tried to make him as comfortable as possible but my nursing didn't do much good. We suspected he might be suffering from some form of dysentery, but we weren't at all sure. We were hesitant to use any of our medicines until we knew what his illness was.

The papaya I found was the only ripe one in the village and I had had to pay two rupees to persuade its owner to knock it down from the tree. I ended up devouring it and mooched about while Ados dozed the day away. There seemed nothing to do but wait for the next day and then struggle the two miles to the larger village of Arughat Bazar, where I thought there should be a medical store, a radio operator or even a health worker.

The following day was Day 25 of our expedition. Ados felt better for his long sleep and managed to hold down sips of rehydration drink. But we weren't in a hurry to move and lazed about for much of the morning, gathering energy for the next short haul.

Eventually I paid our host for his trouble and two hours of very gentle walking along a river bank took us to Arughat Bazar. On the way we saw a beautiful snow peak at the end of the valley and this was a morale boost for Ados who, once we'd arrived, was able to enjoy two glasses of hot milk – his first food for about thirty-six hours. Then, once again, he lay down while I went off to explore the village and search for suitable accommodation.

Scouting a row of decrepit chai houses, I found an old lady squatting beside her wood fire. Calling her 'Amai', the Nepali word for mother and a term of respect for all old women, I asked for a room. A girl who was washing spoons and glasses in a puddle of rainwater came to show me a room that turned out to be her son's. This was a bare attic room with a couple of straw mats and a low, sloping thatch roof. It wasn't a bridal suite by any means, but it was just the sort of space I was looking for. I hurried back to collect Ados.

'Dick came charging back, picked up my bags and excitedly took me round to the old shanty end of town, then with a satisfied sweep of his arm, ushered me into what was nothing more than a wonky old clay hut with a thatched roof. We went out to the back yard where he introduced me to 'Amai', the old woman. She smiled up at me from the pot of rice she was stirring. I looked around the muddy yard littered with bits of old food and chicken shit and I wondered what on earth Dick had landed me in – I needed rest and care, not a dose of ethnic poverty! Then I realised Dick had provided our very own cook and cleaner and what's more, there was also a table we could use. We hadn't had the use of one for four days and that had to be a plus factor!'

I scrabbled through the kind old woman's jars and urns to see what food there was. There was little available, but I directed the woman to cook up a couple of strange foreign dishes such as scrambled eggs and rice pudding. There were also noodles in a savoury sauce which Ados liked best of all and actually ate! I myself still had the runs and from time to time felt a bit nauseous. It was enough to persuade me that Ados might be right. We needed a full day off to rest and recuperate. And take stock.

That evening we analysed our present state, the aims and potentials of our expedition. We had done fantastically well in the first twenty days, poorly in the next five, and now – only a quarter of the way – had come to a standstill. We were dropping way behind schedule.

Of course, we had set the schedule when we knew nothing about the Himalayas. Now we were awake to all the problems and realised that we could never complete the traverse in one hundred days. We could struggle on for months and eventually get to the end, but anyone could do that. What should we do? We could give up now with the very valid excuse that we had been sapped by illness – and with the record from Everest Base Camp to Kathmandu safely secured. Alternatively, we could struggle on and simply collapse wherever we were at the end of the hundred days, returning home as heroic failures who had made the first serious attempt at the one hundred-day traverse. We took the second course. It meant another seventy-five days of known and unknown hardship. We figured it would be like an insufferable term at boarding school.

13

A Day Off

Richard: It was raining – a heavy pre-monsoon downpour, but life went on as usual. A young girl skipped on tiptoe over to the tiny, dilapidated Hindu temple on the corner, shielding her early morning offering of red, blue and green powders, some flowers and a bowl of water. She sprinkled a little outside and entered. A scrawny dog got soaked as it scratched itself apathetically in the middle of the street. A woman, her long blue sari clinging to her skin, passed, balancing a big stone water jar on her hip. Two men in torn shorts rushed by, with wet grey blankets over their shoulders. Bedraggled chickens pecked around in the mud. An empty cigarette packet bobbed around in a puddle, bombarded by the raindrops while the torn pages of exercise books were slowly churned up with the mud, the stones and straw of the main street in Arughat Bazar.

In one of the rooms behind me, children were shouting and laughing. I could hear Amai chiding them. An elderly man came in. His legs were all bone and sinew and the mud formed boots on his bare feet, right up to his ankles. His face was dark brown, his shoulders hunched over his concave chest which quaked as he hacked out a rasping cough. He went through to the back and reappeared a minute later with a short clay pipe shaped like a vase with the stem below the bowl. He smoked and he coughed. Another man appeared and they silently shared the pipe, drawing the smoke through cupped hands.

We lazed away the morning. Then around midday Ados felt better, so we strolled down to the river for some gentle exercise. Since we weren't fighting to make mileage, we actually enjoyed the warmth after the rain. Wandering slowly along the bank brought a whole new perspective to the Nepali scene. Everything is so unhurried: the cows and the buffaloes amble along, the ants 'work to rule' and even the children play leisurely games. Lying on the grass I watched a beetle climbing, one careful step at a time, up the narrowing spire of a leaf. The leaf bends lower and lower under the weight and when the beetle reaches the tip, it swings underneath, hangs suspended, then flops gently to the ground. Not much to write home about, you might say, but that rare close-to-nature feeling which is wonderful.

We watched the village women washing clothes in the stream, slapping them clean against a boulder and laying them out to dry on the river bank. Another woman, half-way up a steep cliff, was cutting green leaves and fodder for her buffaloes. Three men were fishing, throwing their nets in unison into the pools.

Another man carried some buffalo feed across the river from one bank, thick with vegetation, to the other. Two girls hoisted huge wicker baskets piled high with grass on to their heads. Three little children, somewhere between four and ten years old, were collecting firewood in baskets at least a mile from home. We dozed for a while, then headed back into town for a tour of the chai houses and their snacks, the samosas and onion fries which Ados had avoided the past few days, and was now prepared to try again.

By the time we got back to Amai's the thunder was coming up like the old man's cough. We wrote some necessary letters, modified Adrian's sunhat to give him a larger area of shade, strengthened the stitching on our rucksack straps and made a new pair of mittens from Ados' old thermal top, ready for the snows.

At 5 pm it was suddenly and dramatically night-black. In next to no time the rain was coming down in curtains and the street had become a stream. Lightning split the heavens and the thunder practically blew our heads off. Little children went crazy, singing and dancing and pushing each other into the storm. A teenager under an umbrella rolled up his trousers and ran up the street, but the wind turned his umbrella inside out. Everyone, save an old woman bent over her cooking, stopped to watch the storm. It was that impressive.

It stopped as quickly as it had started. The black clouds scuttled away over the horizon and the first sun of the day filtered through. Amai went back to squat by her stove and her daughter picked up a straw handbrush and started sweeping the floor.

I looked at Ados. 'Good job we weren't out today.'

'I dunno,' he said. 'I reckon that it could have been good fun.'

'If we had been out, we would have been miles away now,' I said with a slight dig.

'Well, there's always tomorrow,' said Ados.

Another seventy-four tomorrows, to be exact.

On Day 27 Adrian woke up before me. It was about the first time he'd done so and, for a change, he attended to breakfast. Although rested, he was by no means one hundred per cent and could have done with a longer lay-off. But any suggestion that he wasn't ready would have created some very real animosity in me. I had sought and found something meaningful in our enforced day off, but I was still frustrated by the delay.

So we set off and in six hours reached Gorkha – the place which gave the famous Gurkha soldiers their name. A major hill town with a large, solid monastery, Gorkha provided a large meal which had us staggering to a river valley and another out-of-the-way night stop.

The next morning, Adrian was in trouble again. He had severe stomach ache and couldn't eat anything. This is what I wrote about it:

'Ados is right now deeply involved in another case of nausea and running shits. He's somewhere in the trees and terraces behind. I don't know where but a gang of local school kids do, for they are yelling and screaming and having a whale of a time pointing him out.'

I myself was awaiting a 'call of nature' which, for some time, had come suddenly and urgently a few hours after waking, barely giving me time to drop my trousers. Otherwise, I was fine.

I also felt magnanimous enough to think kindly about the schoolchildren, who often were pests. I was impressed, and saddened in a way, by how clean and smart they were in their school clothes and how obviously keen they were to learn how the world and their watches worked, to talk English and speak about England which they hoped to visit one day.

Their first disillusionment was to try talking to two tired and dishevelled travellers like ourselves who could hardly pluck up the energy to talk civilly to them.

Their second disillusionment would come when they picked up the droppings of western culture. They could only lose in the rat race – lose the things that mattered, the pure simplicity and integrity of their hillside lives.

Some of this thinking was brought on by our visit to Gorkha, a splayed-out shambles notable for all the disgusting noise and construction work of 'progress' going on. But we were also in Intermediate Technology country and were constantly being reminded of the aims of that charity to help the people of places like Nepal to ward off poverty and meet the threats which were undermining their society and environment.

The forecasts for Nepal are, in fact, frightening. It is said that twelve million lives will be at risk in the next decade, unless the rapid destruction of the Himalayan forests is halted and reversed. The huge increase in population whose main fuel is wood (supplemented by dry yak or cattle dung) has brought about the decimation of the trees on which the ecological welfare of the region depends. Unless the forests are maintained, the hills and their terraces might be eroded beyond repair.

One of IT's contributions has been designing and developing new low cost cooking stoves which use one-third less wood. The aim is to help train local potters to produce the millions of stoves needed. The charity is also introducing new wool spinning techniques – just simple adaptations to traditional methods – to help the seven million wool spinners compete better against the large textile mills in the cities.

Another IT programme is to produce tiny water turbines which grind grain efficiently and cheaply. These machines end countless hours of drudgery for village women.

Windmills of IT design pump water for irrigation and villagers. A workshop in Pakistan now uses an IT model that has spread to India, Kenya, Botswana and Egypt, providing clean water for thousands of small farmers, health clinics and rural schools. The charity is involved in almost 240 projects like these in more than sixty countries. Yet it operates on a small annual budget compared with other overseas aid schemes – only about £1.4 million.

Now we were part of an appeal campaign to raise another £250,000. We had a real incentive to help the charity, but the way I saw it, we couldn't run blindly through Nepal.

Following what we called the 'old pack route', we came to Turture, some distance west of Gorkha. Here we had scheduled a visit to the IT-aided hydropower projects, which consisted of a turbine in a ramshackle, shaking shed perched on the hillside. This was connected by various belts and wheels to a seed crusher for oil, a maize grinder for flour, another grinder (not working) and an electricity generator (also not working). Because the water flow was so low at that time of the year, the turbine on its own wasn't sufficient and a smelly, noisy diesel engine was also hooked up to the drive.

Being a perfectionist, I found this project too like a Heath Robinson contraption to impress, but another installation I saw that day reassured me that simple hydro-power was an obvious answer to out-dated time-consuming techniques and an aid to a better way of life.

From Turture, we pressed on heading north.

It was going to be a fascinating stretch. For one thing, the Annapurna massif was up ahead, and we were ready for some more high altitude adventuring. What we couldn't foresee was the effect that Adrian's restoration would have.

On Day 28, he was still recording a list of ailments – 'bad guts, aching back, aching shoulders' – and bemoaning his dreadful performance. One consolation was the state of our finances:

'One thing that makes a materialist like me feel better,' he wrote, 'is that I have checked our money and we appear to be well financed right to the airport. We've got £4 a day each and enough to spare for any problems.'

The following day, Day 29, his health balance was also in credit: 'Oh, how good it is to feel well!' he exclaimed. 'Have walked a full day, felt strong to the end and have been in high spirits. Have only the slightest stomach pangs and my fingers are tightly crossed as I wait for the next dahl bhaat.'

Adrian's renewed interest in life was clearly reflected in these daily entries. They suddenly got more expansive, more optimistic and more humorous. He even looked forward to the days ahead, following the 'pancake trail' – the tourist route around Annapurna. He noted with some relish that we'd be able to get things like chocolate, pancakes and jam.

On Day 30, he *still* felt good', the rain was 'fun' and traipsing up the deep Marsyandi valley, he wondered if he could be in 'the biggest rut in the world'. He decided it was more like the proverbial tunnel from which he could only escape in seventy days time. The thing was that he could now see the light at the end – and would lead his bigger, older, stronger brother towards it.

14

The Pancake Trail to Annapurna

WE WEREN'T travelling at the height of the season but, making our way up the Marsyandi Khola towards Annapurna, we had already met more tourists on the trail than Gurungs (who, for the record, probably number around 5000 people grouped in several villages).

Most of the trekkers would have caught a bus in Kathmandu and travelled west along the plains, south of the old porter's route we had taken via Gorkha, to road villages such as Dumre or Turture. From these places on the Marsyandi river they head north, up the gorge between the Annapurna massif on the left-hand side and Manaslu, another 8000-metre peak, on the right. The Marsyandi leads them round to Manang, a biggish village at 11,500 feet near the river source, where they have a recommended period of acclimatisation. Then, if it's passable, they climb the Thorong La, the gateway at 17,800 feet to the sacred village of Muktinath. From here, the trek plunges south down the Kali Gandhaki – truly the deepest 'rut' in the world – between Annapurna and Dhaulagiri and back to the foothills.

We had hit a bad time. The winter snow on the Thorong La, we were told, still hadn't thawed and only a handful of well-equipped climbing parties had got through in scattered spells of good weather. We were warned that the pass, easy enough in the summer months, was dangerous when it snowed, especially for anyone not properly equipped for a night out. You might say we fitted that category. Our clothes, despite their thermal layer, were hardly adequate for the freezing cold. Our running shoes were useless against the cold and wet and hopeless for a prolonged climb in snow. If we were to get over the pass it had to be a quick zap! up-and-over! Otherwise we faced a six-day back-track and detour around the south of Annapurna. The thought horrified us. It had occurred to us earlier that the southern route was much the quicker one, but the long loop we wanted to run around Annapurna and its three sister summits was, like the visit to Everest, irresistible. Ados simply wouldn't tolerate the short cut – not if it meant missing a snow challenge and one of the most remarkable areas of the world!

So, come what may, we pulled our jackets more tightly round us, lowered our heads against the biting wind, and made for Manang. Much to the delight of my brother, we'd run into snow the day before (Day 31) and I had a great time pathfinding, but by the time we reached Manang the snow was melting fairly rapidly.

Among the tightly packed stone houses we found one proclaiming 'hotel' status and went in to join nine other foreigners who, we discovered, were going to spend three or four weeks on a trip that Ados and I hoped to cover in six or seven days.

'Been here long?' I asked one of them, an American.

'A couple of days,' came the reply.

'Are you heading over the pass?' said Ados.

'No sir, it's not crossable yet,' we were told. 'The villagers say the snows have been heavy and travellers won't be able to get over for a few more days.'

'Are there many others waiting to go?' I asked.

'Quite a few. I'll give it a couple more days and then I'll have to head back down the Marsyandi. I must be back at work a week on Monday.'

He was cutting it a bit fine! Then he said that some Australians, Americans and a Frenchman had set out that day and hoped to get over the next day.

'But where do they stay?' I asked. I'd thought that Manang was the last stop, that there was nothing but ten miles of arid mountain between the 11,600-foot plateau on which we were resting and the Thorong La 6000 feet higher up.

'There's a shack called "Base Camp" near the foot of the pass, about five hours trek from here,' said our informant. 'Two sharp Nepalis sit there with sacks of rice and packets of biscuits waiting for guys like us. They have tea brewing and a big money box because everyone who goes over has to spend the night there. I have also heard there's an old hermit woman who is sometimes to be found in a hut part-way up to Base Camp. She also has food.'

'Do you know where the best route goes?' asked Ados.

'Well, sort of,' offered the trekker. 'I followed up the first part myself yesterday to get some brisk exercise. You keep on the right hand side, round the shoulder above here into the approach valley and stay well up on the right above the headwaters. The actual path is poor. I didn't go far. I think it's simply animal tracks most of the way, then you have to cross back at some point to get into Base Camp.'

His effort faded into vagueness.

Ados turned to me: 'Shall we or shan't we?' he asked.

'What? Get over the pass?' I queried in turn.

'No, dear brother,' he said with a resigned sigh. 'Shall we or shan't we set out now for Base Camp?'

'You do realise that we have absolutely no chance of getting there today? There's only two hours of light left. Unless, of course, all these estimates of four to seven hours are wildly wrong, and that's always a possibility.'

'If we go now, we should get close enough to the pass tonight to have a bash at it tomorrow. Otherwise tomorrow will have to be a reconnaissance and the next day the attempt. We might even stumble on the old woman if she's up there somewhere.'

It was risky, but Ados made sense. We'd done this sort of thing before in Scotland.

'All right,' I said. 'Let's not waste time. Let's go now. We can always bivouac.'

'But we've got no bivouac bag,' Ados pointed out.

'Aw, don't worry,' I said confidently. 'We can get behind a rock, under a stream gully, or in snow hole. We don't need a bivouac bag. And if we're going to go now, let's go! Or we'll waste tomorrow and lose one more day. We can always come back if the weather's really bad tonight.'

I was now wearing two pairs of shoes! The New Balance runners I had picked up in Kathmandu were size eleven, and I usually wore nine-and-a-half to ten. To solve the problem of bigness, I bought a pair of plimsolls in Turture, cut off the toe caps and shoved them into the runners. This had done the trick, thank heavens, because it would have been miserable, even disastrous, for my feet if it hadn't.

Most of the snows around Manang had melted by the time we set out in late afternoon. This created rivulets down the slopes and the paths were slushy and slippery. With a sense of urgency we quickly rounded the mountain shoulder and turned up into the empty valley on the right. We were thrown into shadow as the sun went down and the temperature dropped rapidly. We put on all our clothes except our down duvets – we'd save those for when it really got cold.

Adrian: Both Dick and I realised that it could be dangerous up on the Thorong La, especially if the weather closed in. We would then have to use all the mountain craft we'd absorbed over the years and keep an eye on the other for any signs of weakening. Medically speaking, we were hardly the best candidates for a climbing team, and although I was recovering quickly, Dick's insides were playing up something dreadful. We suspected it might be dysentery.

Richard: Suspected? Suspected, my foot! As far as I could feel and diagnose it *was* dysentery. It had to be, because the morning sickness symptoms, the amount of gas I was letting off and my hasty detours into the bushes looked very much like Giardia. I carried the correct medicine for it, but I was reluctant to start a five-day course of the stuff because one side effect is to bring on extreme lethargy! I couldn't afford that. Besides, I didn't want to start the cure unless I was totally convinced of the cause. My emphatic diagnosis could be wrong!

The alternative was to put up with it, apply a bit of mind over matter. The problem was, the rot was starting to call the tune. My diary records one of these calls the night before:

'One of the closest things to total hell that ordinary mortals can experience must be the rude awakening caused by a distended bowel at one in the morning, when tightly sealed in a deep sleep by thermal underwear, balaclava and a warm sleeping bag. Then to be forced out at minus-three degrees celsius to fumble with wet, freezing shoes and trudge ankle deep in snow to bare one's bottom to the high Himalayan winds for fifteen minutes of protracted stomach contractions is no joke, I tell you.'

If I had to be laid low I would have preferred a less embarrassing complaint, a more romantic and dramatic injury. As we reached for the other end of the grey valley we were in, I had my concentration on a more urgent need – finding a safe place for the night. I was pessimistic about reaching the Base Camp and the signs indicated a long, cold and sleepless bivouac.

As we pressed on, the path petered out and left us guessing the best route along the slopes. We travelled warily, contemplating each boulder, gully and little knoll we came to as a bivouac site. We remembered the position and distinctive features of each 'possible' in case we had to retreat to it in the dark. We prayed that no rain or snow would fall because there were no perfect sites. There weren't even any good sites. All the possibilities were awful, some more awful than others. Then, with our spirits descending as darkness did, we crossed a gully, rounded an inconspicuous knoll, and there, all of a marvellous sudden, was safety! A wisp of smoke rose out of a low flat hut. Obviously the old hermit woman was at home. We entered without a knock.

Inside, the air was thick with smoke and the smell of bodies. As my eyes adjusted to the light of a flickering candle and a glowing fire, I saw faces materialising out of the darkness. Then I could see rucksacks, bags and wood stacked around the walls. We removed our packs and stepped over bodies and blankets towards the middle of the room. After some shuffling of the bodies, we staked our space for the night. There were a dozen of us crammed in the one room, and from the lively atmosphere it was clear everyone was enjoying their trek immensely. We spent an entertaining evening speaking to some Australians, one of whom was a nurse. She confirmed my Giardia diagnosis – oh shit! – so I resolved to start the course of tablets once over the pass.

The food situation was poor – no dahl bhaat, no tsampa. Just potatoes, and we each had a plate, piled so high it impressed Ken, one of the Aussies. He wrote in our log book:

'Adrian and Richard spent the night with us at Leder, above Manang on the Thorong La trail. The bastards ate half our tucker as well as a great plate of spuds – greedy buggers.'

I had to pay for that I guess, for my sleep was disrupted by another race with my bowels by moonlight.

Round about five thirty I gave Ados a first-light nudge and we were up and away in minutes. It was a magnificently clear day, no wind, no clouds, but it was freezing. For practically the only time on the trip, we had to wear our duvet jackets while actually on the go. Ados warmed quickly but I felt cold as we crunched the frozen snow and I settled in behind my brother.

Adrian: My sights were set on the summit of the pass. I felt confident that in this good weather our mountain skills would get us over and I knew that Dick, even in his weakened state, had so much competitive grit and determination that he could get to the top if I could. We made good time in the icy air along the valley, then as we came up towards its head, the first rays of the sun hit us. Within minutes I had to remove my duvet and Dick was noticeably perkier. Blocking the valley ahead stood a massive grey rockface while a big snow gulley led up to the left. This, I decided, had to be the way to the pass and, with any luck, a breakfast at Base Camp. We headed on towards the gully, then spotted footprints in the snow and followed these tracks into a depression in the moraines. There, half buried in the snow, was Base Camp – a low stone-walled tin-roofed shack.

Four well-wrapped Nepalis welcomed us and gave us tea and tsampa porridge. Apparently they'd accommodated about twenty trekkers who left at seven for the 4000-foot climb up the pass. The sun was now bright and the snows still crisp as we followed the trekkers' footsteps away from Base Camp. The glare was intense but we had sunglasses and our versatile Helly Hansen balaclavas pinned tightly across our faces. We were effectively blinkered, and to see anything on the side we had to turn our heads. I enjoyed myself leading the way across the snows and behind me, Dick crunched on, plodding doggedly along in my footsteps.

Richard: I wasn't very interested in where we were, only in reaching the summit. But to give Ados his due, I admired him for leading all the way. I wanted to help but could only follow, my heart racing with the effort and my lungs gasping.

Adrian: With Dick struggling so hard, I became worried that altitude sickness might overtake him and force us to retreat. I knew that I would have to keep an eye on him and not lead him on too fast.

Up ahead, a group of climbers who had started from Base Camp earlier were ascending a steep section of the gully. They were moving very slowly. We gained on them rapidly and I noticed they were all taking only about ten slow steps at a time. Then they'd stop and hang, panting, on their staffs as they tried to catch their breath. We had gone some miles in the very early morning before reaching their starting place, had caught them up and were still moving fast. It was a demonstration of our fitness which surprised us both.

Out on our own, I searched for the optimum route across firm snow, kicking footholds into the crisp surface. The sun had been strong for a number of hours and the crust in places was soft. Consequently, I would suddenly drop through, knee-deep in powdery snow, and struggle for several steps at a time. Our feet were cold and wet but not yet numb. We knew we had to move continuously to keep them warm. It was necessary also to get to the summit before the snows became too soft. This didn't bother me: I was optimistic now that the weather would hold and we would negotiate the pass. While Dick was struggling, I dreamt of the fun I could have if I brought all my climbing gear here. These majestic snows and peaks would be prime candidates for lightweight ascents! I got out the camera to make lightning photo stops. It was the first time since Everest Base Camp that I had been leading the way.

Perhaps, I thought, I'm a mountain man.

Richard: He's not a mountain man, he's a yeti! I was stalking him carefully, step after step. Every time I got close he would sprint off, then stop and wait before going on again. He was totally at home up there. We would see a mound that looked like the top of the pass. He would race up to it. I would plod agonisingly after him only to see him disappear again, his shout reaching me: 'False summit!'

The climb, we discovered, was a mass of false summits but eventually the gradient levelled off and the other side of the world unfolded in front of us. The top of Thorong La! We hugged each other with joy. We'd made it! We'd broken through another barrier and for a few glorious moments we felt as though we were on top of the world. The views matched this feeling. Looking the way we had to go, I got the distinct feeling it was downhill from now on. If only I didn't feel so crappy . . .

15

In the Deepest Rut

AT THE FIRST hostel we came to in the high and holy town of Muktinath, a fat man sat by the door and fingered a pencil.

'Have you a room?' I asked. The man didn't look up. Two men sat hunched over an empty table. There wasn't a flicker of interest.

'Are there any spare rooms here?' I repeated.

The question carried around the pale green room but no one moved. The only answer was the whistle of the wind through the broken window pane. A thin youth in an overlarge pair of battered leather boots dragged himself in from a side door. He clumped across the room and out the other side.

'Is this a hotel?' I demanded. 'If not, what's that sign for? If it is a hotel, then have you beds?'

A shaggy pile picked itself up from the floor and walked out pretending to be a dog. Fatman, at last, turned his face up to me and opened his mouth: 'Full up,' he said in English. And that was that. No more need be said. There was no room at the inn. We left.

Out in the intense sunshine, many people were milling about. A donkey nosed among some rotten vegetables while its driver urinated against the wall. Beside my purple running shoes, a young boy washed dishes in the gutter. A couple of groups sat around their fires drinking tea. Nearby three canvas tarpaulins had been erected as makeshift tents. A mother was breastfeeding her child.

'A chilly business,' I thought. And not just because we were at 12,500 feet and there was snow on the ground. It was a cold town.

A hard-faced man with rough, dark skin, wrapped up in layers of thick woollen overcoats, was strolling across the square. Beside him a Buddhist lama with elegant yak skin boots walked with his hands clasped behind his back and his deep maroon robe tied with a woollen belt. These two, and the chubby red-faced women we saw carrying baskets of heather, were clearly mountain folk raised at this high altitude. In contrast, many of the other men and women were lightly built and finely featured, dressed in bell-bottom trousers and gaudy shirts with plastic lace-up shoes. Two women wore saris. I decided they must come from the foothills or plains far away. They didn't look like locals.

'What's going on here?' Ados asked.

'Goodness knows,' I replied. 'It's like a mortuary in the hotels and a bazaar in the street. Let's ask across there.'

We headed over to a group of strangely dressed people sitting by a wall. Tibetan wool boots, Indian thongs, worn-out trainers, climbing boots, even a pair of African open-toe sandals – we had the lot here. I squatted down and said, 'Hello' to a pale young man on the edge of the group. He flicked his hair back and smiled, saying:

'Hey man, what's the action?'

'I just wondered what was going on here?'

'Oh man, big religious festival tomorrow. Folks come from all over. We're just warming up. Care to join in?' He offered me a drag on a tightly rolled smoke.

'Maybe later, man,' I said in mimicry of the hippie. 'Right now we gotta find a bed.'

'Not a cot in town. Place is stuffed full of Indians. Pilgrims. The doss houses aren't interested. Try the North Pole Hotel at the end of the wall.'

Nearly forty foreign travellers were in town to witness the festivities and all had come up by the recommended path along the Kali Gandhaki past Jomosom, which is as far as many trekkers get. A number we spoke to had never heard of the Thorong La, and only a couple had thought about crossing it.

At the North Pole Hotel, we found a couple of beds, and ordered tea and settled down to up-date our diaries. It had been a long day and it was to be a long evening, for we waited two hours until any food at all was produced and then only half of what we ordered. The cooks were indifferent and the kitchen seemed in disarray. Ados was more frustrated than I. I didn't particularly care because my insides were also in disarray. When we tried going to bed, we found that they had been double-booked and mine had been usurped by a blanket-swathed, barefooted guy and his beloved guitar. Cursing and swearing I laid two sacks out on the floor of the eating room and stretched out in my sleeping bag with my socks on. The night was long and rotten. I tossed and turned and waited for dawn.

Adrian: Dick had a very bad night: cramp, cold feet and bad guts. In contrast, I slept wonderfully. I guess we shall both soon be well and then things will be easy. My only health problem now is a painfully sunburnt lower face from the snow glare yesterday. We had wrapped up our eyes, ears, nose and neck tightly against the high altitude sun on the pass but had omitted to cover our chins, lips and nostrils from the reflected glare. I couldn't stand the pain of splashing water on my face this morning.

Dick was slow to get moving. He muttered on about his diary and this depressing town as we ate a breakfast of porridge and Tibetan bread. I was keen to get away so I told Dick to hurry up.

Outside the town was wakening up in the crisp morning air. Pilgrims squatted in heavy blankets around little fires clasping glasses of steaming chai. A faint murmur came from three lamas who glided ever so smoothly across the lower side of the square. And over by the wall where those left-over hippies had been acting cool last night, a very old woman lay, covered in a heap of rugs. The squeaks from the prayer wheel spun by her husband went out to the wind. I felt sad. Dick had been too harsh on the village when we came in from the mountains last night. We had been jubilant and full of ourselves and greedy for special attention after crossing the Thorong La.

65

But we over-reacted. Had we taken the time, we'd have discovered that Muktinath was, in fact, a fascinating town.

For one thing, we missed the 'auspicious combination of earth, fire and water' that is responsible for the religious importance of the town. Behind a tattered curtain in an ancient temple there are small natural gas jets that apparently 'produce a perpetual holy flare alongside a spring that is the source of the sacred water'. The monastery and these natural phenomena make this ancient mountain kingdom sacred to both Buddhists and Hindus. Needless to say, the area is dotted with ten-foot high stone chortens, white beehive structures customarily painted with the eyes of Buddha who watches over all the world.

By the time Dick came out of the hotel with his pack on his back, Buddha had watched numerous pilgrims journey into town for the day's festival. As we headed out towards the Kali Gandhaki valley and the town of Jomosom, we passed many more on the climb to upliftment.

The oasis of green around Muktinath was soon behind us. We followed a trail into an arid silence, staying well up on the coarse brown expanses to the left of the valley. There were no birds here. Below us angular shadows emphasised sharp gullies gashed into the terrain by centuries of violent flash floods. Around and about us the air was clean, the sky was clear and the sun shone bright. The slopes we were on were as dry and parched as a Bedouin's tongue and I thought of the desert and wadis of Saudi Arabia, of camps with camels and barbecued steaks and the time Karen and I were caught in a sand storm. Dick's dreams, I knew, were on the other side of the world in sailing boats in the Galapagos Islands.

Richard: I couldn't help feeling I'd seen this before. Here were the same sharp slopes and rough rock formations I'd come across among the volcanic cliffs and barren lava flows of the Galapagos. The sun was just as hot, and underfoot was just as dry and rubble-rough. All that was lacking was the screech of swallow-tailed gulls by the sea and the iguanas scampering off into the cacti. And, of course, the island sightseers who would ask: 'What's the name of that mountain?' and I, the guide, who would answer: 'Volcano Darwin.'

Now the tourists were Himalayan trekkers and the answer was 'Dhaulagiri'.

Adrian: Dhaulagiri at 8167 metres is seventy-six metres higher than Annapurna. When the Frenchman Herzog saw it – his first Himalayan giant – far away in the distance, he described it as 'a terrific wall of ice rising above the mist to an unbelievable height, and blocking the horizon to the north for hundreds and hundreds of miles. This shining wall looked colossal, without fault or defect.'

I know exactly how Herzog must have felt. Of all the mountains it was the one that enthralled me most. I had heard of it as the seventh or so in height, but I had no idea of the image it makes on the mind. It's one of those beautiful conical sloped mountains and it absolutely rears, 15,000 feet of mountain, right in front of you, and you're only four miles away from it. To see the summit you've got to tilt your sight to forty-five degrees and even then you can't take it all in. I mean the magnificence of it all. Oddly, it left Dick cold – like a picture postcard, he said.

Although Dhaulagiri was a great challenge and they could see a way to it, the

French opted for Annapurna, and it was another ten years before Dhaulagiri finally succumbed to a Swiss team.

We had had the mountain in our sight since rounding the bend north of Annapurna, and as we jogged down the Kali Gandhaki, it loomed higher and higher.

We were still in the northern semi-desert section of this gorge which glaciers had carved at least a flat mile wide. There is no road along its high sloping banks but the path we were on was wide and easy enough, a route padded by pilgrims, traders and pack animals for centuries. From where we were, the river was a silver sliver slinking this way and that over the shingle. Southwards, we knew, the river would arrive at the edge of the Tibetan plateau and go plunging down narrow gorges to the humid and sub-tropical Himalayan foothills.

We could see a long thin line of porters and their animals crawling slowly over the alluvium below. They had probably left the roadhead nine or ten days ago and had many days march ahead. We were going well and all set to make good time, until we met the caravan and photography put the brake on yet again. The camera takes pictures but pictures take time, effort, energy and they certainly taxed my patience and the fragile working relationship we were running on. I calculated one and a half minutes per snap, 1970 minutes for 1080 snaps so far. That was twenty-seven hours! Ten per cent of our moving time!

Richard: The travellers on the move were exotic and colourful. Good subjects for portraits and wide angles with the donkeys and loads. We snapped shot after shot as each group walked by. Then waiting for the next lot, we snapped the scenery. Each photograph led to much discussion or, if you prefer, argument, as to balance and composition. We also took an age propping up the camera with stones to capture action shots of the two of us. We set the eight-second delay timer going, then ran in front of the lens. My impatient brother found it tedious but the results made all the time and bother worthwhile. Besides, we made Jomosom for lunch.

With perfect timing we reached the village of Kalopani at dusk. We found the lodging of our dreams: warm, friendly, efficient, uncrowded. Two separate beds in our own private room. Good lamps, good food and flowers on the table. We settled down to a couple of relaxing hours before bed. No soft chairs, no books, no telly, no idle banter for us. Relaxation is eating and diary-writing. First things first. We got stuck into a mystery vegetable soup where every spoonful was a surprise, then a superbly flavoured dahl bhaat. A glass of rakshi to celebrate the one-third point of our trip. We had apple pie, creamy hot chocolate – and Ados still managed to stuff in some sweet Tibetan bread. Out came the diaries and maps. We wanted to know where we've been and where we're going.

The maps were of poor quality and such small scale that it was difficult to be precise about our routes. We estimated distances by measuring straight lines along a valley or ridge, then multiplying by a 'wiggliness' factor to make allowance for the bends and zigzags of the paths. We were introduced to this factor in Scotland by our Uncle Hol. It varies from 1 on large flat plains to 1.8 when the path twists madly over steep mountain passes. Total distance to date from Darjeeling was 651 miles and today is Day 34. We were averaging just over nineteen miles per day. Our average had been twenty-five miles per day until we left Kathmandu, when illness slowed us. We had made 147,500 feet of ascent already, climbing over thirty-eight passes. Today we reached another turning point.

The village of Tatopani (meaning 'hot water') which lay a few hours ahead, is famous for its hot springs. These bubble out among the rocks by the river and produce pockets of hot sulphurous air which is thrilling to stand in. To Ados and myself, deeply immersed in an expedition which is the antithesis of pleasure and leisure, Tatopani marked the end of our link to the tourist trail around Annapurna and our entry to remote Nepal. We were eager to reach our stop, have a celebration meal and set out on our own. The trekkers and idle travellers turn left for Pokhara but we headed right, towards the 'wild west'. Five hundred miles of it!

As we neared Tatopani, I was so engrossed in what lay ahead that my concentration lapsed. I caught my toe under a stick and went tumbling to the ground. I took the fall on my hands and luckily received no injuries. This was only the third fall of the trip for me. Ados had gone down twice. You might say one fall every 250 miles on very rough paths was a good record but we couldn't afford to become careless because one bad fall would stop us. Here, still on the Pancake Trail, help would come within the hour. But in west Nepal, help could be many days away.

In Tatopani the chai houses swarmed with trekkers and tourists, so we found ourselves a bench and a moderately clean table on which to spread our paperwork. This was our last point of close contact with the western world for the next twenty days, and we intended to make good use of the trekkers as mail carriers. So we allocated some of our lunchtime to chatting up prospective carriers and targeted in on a friendly English couple. They'd been travelling for a year and were a few more months from home. We wondered how on earth they could afford the time! They agreed to take our mail and our precious diaries and we were grateful. Then we slipped out of Tatopani, breaking our rule on no carrying of food. We took a bar of chocolate.

Dick and a yak herder enjoy an evening in the nomad's camp on Tibetan plateau in the cold of 13,000 ft. He is preparing a chapati to cook on the fire. *Day 79.*

Ados (*left*), Dick (*right*), wearing Gore-Tex jackets and snow-glare protection at 18,000 ft on the Shingo La, Lahoul-Spiti. *Day 79.*

Tibetan villagers digging foundations for a house. Zanskar, 11,000 ft. *Day 81.*

A Tibetan carpenter in Padum, Zanskar. *Day 82.*

Old lady making Tibetan salt tea for us in Zanskar, 10,000 ft. *Day 83.*

Dick and Lobsan Ringen discuss route plans by means of pebbles at 14,500 ft on the Pensi La in Ladakh. Our conventional Western maps in the foreground. *Day 84.*

Head lama entertains us to salt tea and tsampa in his cell at Ringdom Gompa, Ladakh, 13,000 ft. *Day 84.*

Kashmiri nomads. *Day 90.*

Typical meal of rice with a lentil soup (dahl bhaat)

Dick (*left*), and Ados (*right*), as adventurers.

Dick quickly leads Ados up past yaks on a Nepalese trade route.

Dick leads Ados up a stepped trail in Nepal.

Mani (prayer) stones carved by pilgrims, and white Buddhist prayer flags all bearing the prayer 'Om Mane Padme Hum'.

16

An Accident

Richard: Remote Nepal engulfed us instantly. As if to prove we'd left the beaten track we stopped at a place you can hardly call a village: more a mud pit with seven reed and thatch huts. Here a man agreed to put us up for the night. He beckoned us into his hut and we sat down on a reed mat, back to back, to prop each other up. The villagers crept in to view us. I ignored them and opened my diary to capture the day. The children turned to statues, watching me with big eyes. The silence was so intense I could hear my pencil on the paper. I looked up and through the children when the lady brought us two brass bowls of tea. I wrote some more. The crowd seemed mesmerised. Then I lowered my pencil, raised my head and winked at the boy who squatted close on my left with a stick in his hands. He grinned tentatively and looked round at his friends as if to ask their support. Then, as I smiled, their eyes lit up and in a trice they were laughing and chattering and teasing the boy with the stick. Rather embarrassed, his look seemed to say: 'Excuse my friends, they're easily excited.'

The contrast between this and the moneyed society and comparative luxury of the trekker trail which we had left behind at Tatopani was dramatic. Here simple reed mats replaced beds; there were neither tables nor chairs. The flicker of an oil lamp lit our supper. Instead of a menu we were offered a bowl of rice but it came with real sincerity. So different from the discourteous, inconsiderate commercialism of the tourist areas. We had broken free from all that and the indifferent trendy trekkers who, for all the genuine guys among them, had polluted a once simple way of life.

Adrian: Dick was in his element once more. Down to the earth again and sweeping the air with his generalisations and hard inflexible opinions which he can form after the briefest experience of people and places. He decided after the crowded tourism of Namche Bazar and Kathmandu that he was going to hate all trekkers and the tourist industry they create. He then extended it to include all foreigners and everything to do with them. I shared some of his feelings and irritations about our fellow Westerners but, in all fairness, I couldn't see how he could compare so favourably the squalor of this wicker hut and the uneducated people who scuttled around us with the English-speaking trekkers and the comforts of the Pancake Trail we left behind that morning. I looked forward to those comforts, a proper bed, good apple pancakes and fried noodles, shops. But Dick Crane, the masochist, obviously wanted it hard all the way.

When Dick woke me the next morning, I was keen to be away and fretted while he bandaged his blistered heels. Then we set off at a good pace through warm dense vegetation. The canyons of the Kali Gandhaki, at this end only 3000 feet above sea level, were dramatic.

Our trail wound its way among the trees and over the rock piles beside the river. When the banks petered out and the river became a torrent in a gorge, the trail had to detour over the offending cliff, sometimes up solid rock steps and sometimes through three-sided tunnels that had been cut into the walls of the canyon. The roofs of these tunnels were so low we could barely stand up straight. Frequently we came across sections littered with rock fall.

Picking our way down among boulders and loose rocks to a small stream gully, something came from nowhere and struck me, thump, full square on the top of my head. I had no idea what had happened. Like Hercules, I felt as though the sky had fallen on me. I opened my eyes and looked up to see my brother sprinting away from me.

Richard: I heard a dull thud and a cry and spun round to see a rock bouncing off the path as Ados crumpled in a heap. My first reaction was to sprint to safety in case other rocks fell. We couldn't afford to have both of us injured! At the same time, I yelled 'run!' and, turning again, I saw him lift himself up and stagger towards me. I put a concerned arm around him and we sat down.

'How do you feel?' I asked.

'Not too bad. It could be worse,' he replied.

'Here, let's take a look.'

'No, it's all right. I'm just a little stunned.' He put his hand on his head to feel the bruise. 'AArggh!' he exclaimed as he pulled away blood-covered fingers.

I then examined his matted curls but couldn't make out wound from mess. It was obvious his hair needed cutting away if the wound were to be cleaned. I decided we needed assistance and, supporting Ados on my shoulder, we headed back along the trail to Shahashbadhara, the village we had just left.

We were in luck because the village came up with a pair of scissors and antiseptic lotion. The welfare worker only came on weekly visits, so 'Doctor Crane' took charge. I cut away the hair around the wound, swabbed it with antiseptic lotion. Thankfully I found it to be only a shallow cut though one-and-a-half inches long. But, under it, the swelling was already acute and we were worried that his skull might have been fractured. We'd have to wait and see. The nearest medical help was 3 days trek away. I then shaved a clean patch on either side of the wound and fixed a single butterfly plaster across it to act as a stitch. I covered it loosely with cotton wool and Ados put his balaclava on to keep that in place and to frustrate the flies.

'You'd better rest up a bit,' I said, and arranged for us to spend a night in a house.

Adrian: Dick did a good job on my head and I hoped, in my gratitude, that I could do the same for him if anything happened to him. At one o'clock in the morning I woke and was sick. Dick got up to light a candle and attend to his patient and started wondering whether I was showing signs of delayed shock, overeating, or early symptoms of a fractured skull. Fortunately, it didn't seem too serious next day. I even got stuck into a breakfast of chapati, fried egg, and roasted corn but I poured the awful tea over the balcony. I was actually feeling fitter than Dick, who woke in a poor state. He had started his dysentery treatment the day before and complained of feeling weak and nauseous. Frankly, we were very lucky that he hadn't been hit because, in his rotten state, it might have been far more damaging.

Richard: On Day 38 we climbed up the eastern side of an 11,500-foot pass to escape from the drainage of the Kali Gandhaki and get to the headwaters of the Uttar Ganga which flow past Dhorpatan in a westerly direction. It was a long climb up through rhododendron trees, dead wood, moss-covered stones and a swirling mist. All was silent save for the nauseating sound of my brother sucking cold chapati. The slate grey stony path was littered with rhododendron flowers and Ados was in high spirits, imagining marching up there with Bilbo Baggins to meet the Hobbits.

Adrian: The top of the pass was a hilly plateau shrouded in cloud. Dick and I argued over our position on the map and the best compass direction to take. We followed a compromise route down a narrow valley which, happily, opened out into the spacious upper valley of the Uttar Ganga. We moved through pine forests in the clearing mist and met a man grazing horses in a scene like a Hollywood Western.

Dhorpatan turned out to be nearly three hours further away than we had thought, at the top of the pass, and we sighted the first few huts in failing light. From the size of its name on our map we had expected Dhorpatan to be a more solid village than it turned out to be. In fact, it was a cold and dreary place, its dwellings spread wide across the valley.

Richard: We spent the night in a hut used for storage that smelled like an abattoir. It was full of dried meat, piles of yak fur, animal skins, dirty pony saddles, harnesses and blocks of rancid fat. When I woke, I felt as though I had slept inside my own stomach.

By way of a surprise, Ados had got up first and was tucking into a vast breakfast: tsampa, chapatis, butter, sugar, fried egg. He was really into food, attacking each meal like it was his last.

'I think you must have worms,' I said. And he didn't even argue, but actually pondered the question in his diary.

'Have I got worms?' he asked himself.

We went down a wide grassy valley and passed no people for three hours. We stopped for a rest in a deserted village and noted how the warm hillside resembled a dale on the Pennines in July. Then we went on until a goatherd on the hillside yelled at us as we rounded a bend in the valley. The man indicated that there was no way through the forest we were entering. The route he pointed out necessitated a one-mile back-track to a flimsy wooden bridge, so we ignored his gestures and moved off into the forest.

He was right, of course. It was nearly impenetrable, but like fools we fought on. Then suddenly the slope fell away and we slithered and slid down rough crags among the pines to the river below. The water ran fast and looked deep so we searched for a safe ford. Unable to find one, we removed our shoes and socks and stepped cautiously into the freezing river. The rocks underfoot were slippery and covered in algae and the torrent threatened to up-end us. Fortunately, it was only knee deep and we kept our balance but it was a terrifying crossing nonetheless. On the other side we told ourselves we'd learned a lesson: don't go where the locals fear to tread.

A few more hours of struggle on empty bellies took us through pine forests on mountainsides devoid of people and terraces, and then around and down another corner to a village shack where we asked for food. Without waiting for it to be produced, we rummaged around the family's sacks and urns, then roasted corn and beans and boiled up tea and a cornflour sauce. The villagers brought down an ex-Gurkha from his house on the slopes to see us. He was a revered member of the community, had served in Burma, India, Nepal and England, and now supported his family with an army pension.

He was astonished that we had come from Dhorpatan the way we did. He was even more astonished that we had neither food nor camping equipment, and insisted that our porters must be hidden outside or lagging behind with all our goods. I still don't think he fathomed what we were about as he waved us on to Taka, the nearest big village.

17

The Fifty-Day Trip Across Nepal

ON DAY 40, we left Taka, an ancient, untouched, crowded, stone, wood and straw town. We had come down from the high mountains and set our sights for Mahendrenagar, the Nepal/India border town, about twelve days away past Jajarkot and Dailekh. For the first few days we followed the banks of the Sani Bheri River.

In heat approaching 100°F, Adrian lost some of his drive and had to soak his hat in the river at frequent intervals to cool himself down. We had been told the people of West Nepal were suffering a food shortage but finding food didn't turn into a serious problem. We now knew that we could *always* get a meal of 'stodge'. I don't think that we ever deprived anyone else of a meal because every village had its own storeroom of local produce and we were only two people visiting for one mealtime. Along the Sani Bheri we were also treated to fish. One evening I accepted and swallowed a hitherto untried raw delicacy: a small blood sac from the entrails of a river fish.

Shortly before reaching Jajarkot, we crossed the wide deep river in a dug-out canoe – the first non-foot transport we'd used since crossing the Arun, way back in East Nepal.

The two-rupee ride was superb, only us two, and the joke was that the boatman's son who ferried us over had no change for our five rupee note. Prompted by the gesticulating going on, the boatman jumped in and swam across the river to us! Father and son then walked off to get change, leaving us resting, feet up, in the dug-out. They were gone so long we thought what-the-heck, they've taken our money, and so we set off. The next thing we were stopped by shouts and the arrival of a child who had run after us with our three rupees change. I was immediately sorry I'd distrusted the ferryman and drew the moral from the incident that everyone here was kind and truthful. We just found them difficult to understand!

In Jajarkot, we were led to the Chief District Officer who, speaking good English, advised us on the routes up ahead and gave us an instant course in local custom. I made student-like notes:

'Society here is based on the "joint family system". Male line, blood family lines, are the over-riding factor. One man has a number of kids and all sons are devoted to him and "live" in his house until he dies. On death, goods are equally divided among all sons, though a very recent amendment to Nepali law dictates that unmarried women over thirty-five also get a share. Farm areas thus get divided up and plots get smaller and smaller. In the old days this created no problem, for waste land could be utilised but now the thumbscrews are on. A son apparently has the right to tell his father at any time to give him his share, but this rarely happens.

'Farmsteads are measured, not by the actual surface area, but by the "quintals" (one quintal is equal to one hundred kilograms) of corn or rice they produce. This depends on soil quality, irrigation and closeness to transport. Land which can produce one quintal changes hands for about 3000 rupees (£150 sterling).'

We had to go on even though I enjoyed philosophising with the District Officer. But we were slowed up by my dysentery.

'As we get slower, I wonder if we are falling into the category of walkers, rather than runners,' Adrian complained. He was finding this part of the traverse a bore and could not work up any enthusiasm for the race. We both hoped that a change of environment and food once we reached India would improve our morale.

Getting to India would not be that simple. The trunk routes are terrible. They're fine between close villages but may as well be called non-existent in scrub and forest.

Nor did our lack of language help. Asking the way invariably involved us in long and frustrating episodes. To add to our confusion, the Nepalis made virtually no use of hands to communicate. I decided it was because it must be bad manners to point, and I muttered away in my diary:

'It is impossible to get someone to indicate clearly which of two routes is correct. One merely discovers that the route lies generally in this or the other hemisphere.'

Despite the frustrations, we continued to make progress – Mahat, Rukumkhot, Balachaur, Radigaon, Jajarkot, Phumne, Dhercola, Dailekh – were put behind us.

I couldn't seem to shake off my physical problems. I was passing blood and decided I also had worms.

Adrian confirmed in his diary how good it felt to be the stronger for once. He now looked forward to their fiftieth day – the half-way mark whatever the outcome – and approached it in good spirits. The temperature reached 109°F in the shade at midday, so hot that one is continually covered by a thin film of sweat. Adrian copied the local's example and bought an umbrella for forty-five rupees – the largest purchase of our expedition so far – and its shade countered his sun problem. At one tea halt he was even relaxed enough to try a local leaf-rolled cigarette but coughed on the experiment. Then, at Chisapani (meaning 'cold water'), he bought a comb, which said something about the mood he was in even though he only used it once before giving it away.

Travelling down beside the strong Karmali River, we once again felt we were getting somewhere. We had only one more pass before descending to the plains. We were even able to appreciate the country around us, noting what a pleasure it was to sleep under the stars, how intense the background noise of insects was, how sculpted the buffaloes' backsides were. We saw a large, raucous troupe of monkeys, bright blue birds, dung beetles pushing their balls of dung along and marijuana weeds growing everywhere. We saw a big red run slipping into a jungle sea. Memories being created.

At one memorable halt, Adrian sat outside a hut on a bench with two old men, reciting stories of his boyhood while I, inside, leaned against the wall and listened in a wallow of nostalgia.

74

Down to earth from such rare moments of pure relaxation, we had to plough on – another few miles to the next rest, a day's march to another nightstop, another night plagued by jungle mosquitoes. Days saturated in heat – with temperatures, according to Adrian's all-purpose wristwatch, well over one hundred degrees.

By Day 48 we were on the track to Mahendrenagar. We had proved our method of travel was feasible and now only had to carry on for fifty-two more days.

At Rajipur, despite recurrent dysentery and infection, we were still pressing on – Day 49. The next day, we celebrated Day 50, 1000 miles from Darjeeling. But the Indian border was near, and when we entered India again we would be able to claim, with solid satisfaction, the fastest east-west foot traverse of Nepal. In and out and right across the country in less than fifty days.

But we had one more night to go, as it happened, a night quite different from all the others. A night in which we were treated as 'sahib' VIPs.

After following the road through jungle country, we came across a two-tent road builders' camp near Ataria.

Only four men occupied the construction camp when we arrived. They cooked mountains of rice that had our stomachs rumbling in disbelief. Then, just as we started attacking the food and enjoying the peace of a tropical night, two trucks rolled up with nearly twenty more men back from work.

Come bed-time the foreman offered us the only bed, which we accepted gratefully and while Ados and I lay down, closer than brothers, the road workers, seven in our tent, sardined themselves around us on dirty sacks.

In the morning, the Cranes humped their packs and waded across the river that ran beside the camp and tramped for Mahendrenagar.

18

Into India

TANAKPUR JUST across the border in India, was a time for a recap. We'd covered 1000 miles across Nepal, climbed 185,000 feet over 45 passes in temperatures ranging from sub-zero to 109 degrees. We had stayed about 23 nights in ordinary homes, invariably on the floor or on a terrace, one night with porters on a river bank, one night at a construction camp, one night rough, and the balance of about 26 nights in 'hotels', most of which hardly surpassed the category of 'hut'.

On three days – at Kathmandu and Arughat Bazar, we had clocked no miles. Otherwise, we took about five million steps between us to get across Nepal, averaging more than 50,000 steps each a day, over all kinds of terrain but mostly rough, and in parts so treacherous that, even had we been well, it would have been out of the question to try running.

Now we were off into north-west India, and it was a different world. Tanakpur wasted no time in impressing the point on us that Mother India was an insatiable consumer. Our reaction was not far removed from Alladin's amazement in the treasure cave.

We'd gone for thirty-two days without electricity, and suddenly to arrive in a place all lit up with bright lights and noisy with transistors was quite stunning. Fans, fridges, deep freezes, newspapers, book shops, sweet shops, tobacconists, restaurants with ten different courses on offer, fruit stalls with twenty different fruits, bikes and combustion engines and tarmac trade routes into the hills – India seemed to have the lot. In Nepal we saw kids kicking balls of rag and straw. Just over the border, the footballs of Indian kids were genuine plastic.

Out of Tanakpur we were heading for a rendezvous with Intermediate Technology and our equipment dump at Kausani, the first Himalayan town we'd visited after our arrival in Delhi. That time we had made the haul to Kausani by bus but now we faced an uphill slog on foot. Only seventy miles away by the proverbial crow measurement, the distance is about twice as long because of the way the road bends. It was therefore our intention to cut across the hills where possible.

Our first marker was Sukidhang, six miles due north of Tanakpur on the flat and fifteen miles by road. Our path reduced the distance to eleven miles and by the time we'd covered it, we were back in the hills, once more climbing a roller coaster route – from Sukidhang at 3500 feet, we went to Dhoun (elevation 5000 feet), to

Banlekh (6000 feet), and Katikhan (approximately 7000 feet), then on to Davidhura and up and down to Mornaula, Dhaura, Lamgora and Almora.

Our path-finding skills were tested to the full. At one point we persuaded an educated young man to map a route to Almora and, faced with a blank page, he started from a point right in the middle. Moving out to the right he had reached the end of the page after three towns and had to turn his route up the edge, then around and back across the top to reach Almora. He then crammed in an alternative route close to the first, and the main north-south motor road was given an unexpected twist into another corner. But by that time it no longer mattered. We were already lost.

No one seemed able to indicate land masses, rivers, ridges or valleys. Distances were entirely conjectural and compass points beyond comprehension. One explanation for the locals' ignorance of the sort of distances we were interested in was that they seldom walked more than five or ten miles, usually taking a bus if they had to go any further. They advise the long-distance trekker to do likewise, to follow the bus route or not to bother.

We were both anxious to get over our blundering with short cuts and reach Kausani, from which we would embark on a more regular route. But, at the same time, we were obviously stimulated by the challenge of the 'foot' paths and our frustrations were more than cancelled out by our lucky breaks, such as the path we found on the way to Katikhan. It bypassed numerous road bends and turned a sixteen kilometre hike into one of only six.

Relatively speaking, we were also going through a period of reasonable health. Our moods continued to fluctuate between being depressed or cheesed off and being quite light hearted, capable of bursting into hysterical, stomach-aching laughter at some inexplicable joke or other.

We were even getting used to being the centre of attraction each time we stopped at a tea house and went through our almost customary routine. This involved stepping defiantly to the fire and taking over the tea making operation. Our recipe was simple – four glasses of water, half a glass of milk, one-and-a-half teaspoons of sugar and one teaspoon of tea. The locals watched fascinated: once we had fifty spectators. There were never any women in the crowd. When we passed them on the trail, they would quickly get out of our way (children would flee), and from a distance, stand and stare at us as we walked out of their lives.

Our contact with the men was intimate. In Gazhlekh we shared a room with five of them, all heavy smokers. No windows, the only opening – the door – was firmly shut, and what with the kerosene lamp and cigarettes, me farting with Giardia and seven of us breathing, the small black room grew hot and smelly very quickly. But we slept deeply, waking early with the light trying to squeeze through the crack under the door. Next thing, there were five red cigarettes glowing in the dark and the room was alive to a dawn chorus of coughs and splutters and full-blown, deep-delving, lung-clearing, retches. They were all at it, coughing and spitting into the corners of the room.

We were up and out in no time, heading through beautifully fresh and misty fir tree forests, past fruit orchards to breakfast in Davidhura. The grass and flowers were thick with dew and the hedgerows rich with rhododendrons. It was pleasant going but I grew tired and Ados, with his high-frequency stride, left me standing.

Adrian: We woke up on Friday the 13th feeling lucky. We had traipsed miles into the previous night trying to find a bed and, guided by a local, eventually arrived at a place on a steep ridge actually overlooking Almora, the capital of the region. It lay glittering with electricity on an opposite hill. In the morning I could see it, like another Darjeeling, from my sleeping bag. It was only about an hour away.

Climbing up to Almora in a swelling flow of people was a rather Biblical experience for me. At least I was able to imagine what it must have been like for the ancients tramping up to Jerusalem. Thus inspired, we entered the busy and crowded town where spiritual feelings gave way once more to the material. I found a bank, cashed $100 and £160 worth of travellers cheques to take us to one hundred days, went to the post office and ended up, inevitably, in front of a menu.

We wandered out through the streets of Almora in roughly the right direction and landed on a very pleasant old path that dropped through woods to the river valley where we rejoined the main road. Almost immediately we came across a lovely surprise – a milestone or, if you prefer, a kilometre mark. It said thirty-six km to Kausani. Without straining ourselves we could be there for lunch the next day. And since we'd be stopping there over night, that meant two consecutive easy days – very useful for our health.

Above all, I was looking forward to contact with the 'outside' world. Hopefully there would be post from home. The following day we entered Kausani and with growing excitement made for the post office. There was no news for us! Nothing from home, IT, Michèle or Karen. Damn! That was a let down.

Richard: I was tired and cheesed off when I should have been jubilant at reaching another equipment dump. The village seemed much bigger – more developed, with more shops and paths – than it did in February, after Delhi. But it hadn't changed. I had.

Before when we came into rural India we were first-time visitors. We were struck then by its ramshackle character, its unpainted houses, the wooden shanty shacks, piles of refuse alongside the road, wonky tables, broken chairs, dirty dishes and the flies. People in rags.

With my eyes opened by the other, poorer, parts of the Himalayas, I now discerned a more competitive, commercial atmosphere about the place – in the choice of foods it offered, the shoes on people's feet, its viable transport system, post office, electricity and telegraph wires. And none of this did I find particularly novel or attractive. I wasn't even moved by the scenery, all that grandeur which had so impressed us and made me feel so romantic. Instead, I was once more under the influence of my load of negatives, and at odds with myself and the people.

We had been trailed out of Someshevar after breakfast that morning by ten teenage boys. They yapped at our heels, hurling their 'hellos' and limited supply of English words at us. They were obviously trying to provoke a reaction and it was an exercise in self-control to stop myself shouting back at them or 'accidentally' lashing out with a stiff arm.

78

We made our way to the Anashakti Ashram where at least a man called Gupta remembered us, sort of, and showed us to a room with – at last – two beds! But we also had water on tap, a loo en suite and electric light. We inspected the Christmas-like parcel we'd dumped there and were satisfied to find more Indian money – about £60 worth, writing paper and envelopes, spare medicines, shirts, underpants, soap and razor, more maps and a bar of chocolate.

There were no decent socks, no sewing kit, no heel pads and no spare shoes to replace our NBs which were somewhat poorly after their hard work. A surprise luxury was a couple of ties! These we actually put on with our clean shirts in the hope that a bit of sprucing would lift our morale. Little did we know that this was going to soar. That moment Margaret Percy walked in.

Her arrival made Ados positively effusive: 'How terrific to see the girl,' he wrote. 'Suddenly we are no longer two forgotten travellers but part of a team in London, Delhi, Kathmandu . . . What's more, Margaret has a long telex from Steve Bonnist with good news about funds and publicity and requests for Coronation and Everest anniversary messages. It's such an uplift! Everything is suddenly so good!'

She had apparently gone to some lengths to track us down, travelling through the night from Delhi to catch us.

Adrian in particular thrived on conversation with her. He revelled in the dinner that night and the chat that fairly zapped along.

'India has an infrastructure but she sure as hell can't use it,' said Margaret. Adrian liked that line enough to keep it in his diary.

Another guest at dinner was David Hopkins from the Lakshmi Ashram who told us about a west-east traverse of the Himalayas – the first we'd heard of it. He had apparently walked part of the way with Sunderlal Bahugana who crossed the foothills in stages from Srinigar in Kashmir to Nagaland in far north-east India. Walking to further the cause of Chipko, a Himalayan conservation movement, Bahugana left Srinigar in May 1981. By June he had reached the Himachal Pradesh region where he stopped to allow the monsoons to pass before starting again in September. In December he stopped at Kathgodum in Uttar Pradesh and set off once more late in the following February. He reached Siliguri in June 1982, had another break until September, and arrived in Nagaland in January 1983. A truly marathon performance.

Typically, I recorded these details the moment I got back to the Ashram from our very pleasant evening out. I was up at 5.30 the next morning despite the latish night.

There were so many things rushing around my head. I simply had to catch some and put them down on paper before they were lost forever. I needed to reflect on my behaviour the night before, and how my brain had wound down in the weeks we'd been beyond the cultivated chatter of Europeans. I wrote:

'I find it incredibly difficult to keep pace with the conversation. Last night I found that topics were finished before I had even cottoned on to them, let alone started thinking about them. In all fairness, an inability to change from the subject foremost in my mind is not a new problem for me but I do seem to have slowed down considerably. Ados, however, has quickly stepped back into high-speed conversation.'

In Kausani it was necessary to try to map out the rest of the traverse – actually start planning for the end. At our current speed, a hundred days would take us close to Kargil or Srinigar in Kashmir. This, we reasoned, would be a quite acceptable place to finish. Arlene Blum had stopped at the Lamayuru monastery near there. Elaine Brooks and her British Trans-Himalayan Traverse team were planning to stop at Leh. The Indian Army team must also have stopped in the north-west corner of India because they wouldn't have been allowed to cross into Pakistan.

Our problem was that if we stopped at Kargil, we would have failed to traverse all fourteen of the 8000-metre peaks – and this we had set our sights on as the purest traverse. In order to notch the fourteenth, Nanga Parbat, we'd have to reach Gulmarg – twenty road miles west of Srinigar and about 150 to 200 road miles beyond Kargil. That could be as much as another seven to ten days. And the question was simple – was it worth while extending the one hundred day limit we'd set? It was a dilemma. If we didn't extend the time, we wouldn't complete the traverse. If we completed the traverse, we'd go beyond the time.

All we could do was carry on. Faster. And see what happened.

19

Days Out Of the Diaries

Day 58:
Baijnath, Uttar Pradesh
(Very near Kausani)

We waved goodbye to Margaret Percy as she sped off in her taxi to Delhi. We watched our link with the Western world disappearing in a cloud of exhaust fumes. Afterwards we sat on the step of a smoky black chai-shop, our feet in the litter and slime of the Indian gutter.

We felt small and isolated. Like two small boys with our two small bags, deported and deserted in the middle of countless millions of square miles of mountain . . .

Day 59:
Gwaldam (6000 feet)

In pretty good spirits. Not even riled by the staring crowds. News from home has convinced us we're on the right track. This section to Manali has a new and different feel to it. It can't be too bad because it's not that long.

Tharali: 1600 hours

The main Indian footpaths are of a high standard. Usually six foot wide, they are lined by dry stone walls and run along level valley bottoms or cleave up the passes. They have been painstakingly paved with cobbles and rock and although no longer used so heavily because of the modern road they are in much better nick than even the busier paths of Nepal.

We've just taken a photo of the sores on Ados' legs and hands. They are insect bites which he has scratched open and now, instead of healing, they are swelling and spreading. It could be blood poisoning. I worry that this, coupled with his present spurt of diarrhoea, might make him force another recuperative day off.

Kulsari: 1930 hours

The local school teacher has taken charge of us. We are marched from shop to shop and fired with a lot of questions. He slips in one about how much alcohol we drink. (In Baijnath there were at least two liquor stores where the bottles were all marked

'For Medicinal Purposes Only'. I thought there must be a lot of ill people there!) But it turns out that alcohol for pleasure is banned by the Hindu religion.

Food is so cheap. Fifty pence for a meal of curry and rice or chapatis – as much as we can eat. Five pence for a cup of tea. Some foods match English prices: eight p for a quarter pint glass of milk, twenty p for a half-size packet of cheap biscuits, thirty or forty p per pound for fruit, eggs seven p each or forty-two p a half dozen.

Day 60:
Kulsari: 0530 hours

Ados usually sleeps these nights in socks, Gore-Tex trousers, thermal top and jacket draped over his face, lying on top of his sleeping bag. It's his compromise to beat the insects and the heat. I'll try it. But I have another worry now – my left big toe has finally asserted itself. It is sore and swollen. And we're supposed to be heads down and rushing for Manali.

On the road to Karnaprayag: 0730 hours.

Four of the most sacred sites in the Hindu religion are located in this fascinating area of the Himalayas and as much as we would like to visit them, they're too much of a detour – a seven day excursion away. Many of the legends, myths and traditions basic to the Hindu faith derive from this Gharwhal region and the life-giving rivers they spawn are venerated by the faithful. One of the three most important Gods, Shiva, is believed to live in the mountains – his throne is on Mount Kailas, north of us and inaccessible in Tibet. It's a remarkable mountain, sacred to both Hindus and Buddhists and the source of the Indus which goes left from one flank, and the Brahmaputra to the right.

The holy Ganges, 'Mother Ganga', also rises in this region, spouting from the 'cow's mouth', more than 10,000 feet above sea level below the peak of Gangotri. In a few days we will cross the head streams of the holy river, heading for the Sutlej River and the watershed of the mighty Indus.

Lodhwar: 1500 hours

I'm going to have leg extensions fitted to my shorts for greater protection against flies, but more important, as an attempt to stop so many locals gaping at me in short trousers. Dick thinks I'll look just as odd and they'll stare at me anyway.

We have finalised the route to Manali. It's about 330 path miles and about 40,000 feet of climbing. We have travelled 173 path miles from Tanakpur in eight days, so by our calculation (including double-time for climbing) we should be in Manali in fifteen-and-a-half days time. On the seventy-seventh day. At a rate of, say, twenty-three miles a day, we could reach Gulmarg in ninety-nine days. No wonder I'm optimistic. I've even been singing!

Our biggest worry is that, if we succeed, we may have to think of an even crazier project to defeat ourselves!

Day 61:
Karnaprayag
(At the junction of the Alaknanda and the Pinder rivers)

This is something of a 'cowboy' town and notable for the numbers of women in the street. Just about the only women we have seen around the smaller hill villages have been in the fields.

We also have here the added attraction of the Hindu Sadhus, the devotees with long beards, scraggly hair and friendly eyes who roam the country visiting religious shrines. They carry only a loin cloth or wrap-around gown, sometimes a blanket and a stick, a brass pot and a handful of prayer beads or bangles.

We slept at the Dharamsala last night, a wrecked remnant of the Raj, which is now a doss house for wanderers. We slept with about fifteen Sadhus on the concrete walkway of its cobbled quadrangles and at 5.45 we were all up and cracking with the pilgrims coughing like hell as they performed the ritual of the first cigarette.

Dick's toe doesn't look good so we'll take it slowly. We just follow the track. Twisty but level – a lot of friendly Sadhus, no Europeans, a few monkeys. Hills are scarred by rock falls and new roads. I put 300 rupees in a shirt pocket in case my pack gets stolen. All the stories we've heard about bandits revive in me and I feel insecure.

Khankra: 1845 hours

We've seen three sunsets today as we travel up and down the paths chiselled into the near vertical valley walls. My record is five sunsets one evening when, on a silly exercise, I pushed and carried my bike for ten miles across the Lake Fells from Langdale over Scafell to Borrowdale. Ados remembered seeing two sunrises once, cycling through France, the first at the top of a mountain, the second from the town below.

We also passed a memorial stone where Jim Corbett on 1 May 1926 shot the 'Man-eater of Rudraprayag' – a tiger reputed to have killed 300 people!

Lilacs are in bloom! But why didn't they plant fruit trees instead? There are also cacti, prickly pears and many tree ferns in the forests. And marijuana plants, more numerous than nettles. They started appearing again near Almora – giant weeds six foot high!

Day 62:
Still at Khankra: 0600 hours

We went to bed shagged out at 9 pm. The chai shop owner cleared his upstairs room for us and lent us a petrol lamp in a whisky bottle. The night was warm and stuffy so we lay down on our sleeping bags. Within minutes I started scratching. And I scratched and scratched and scratched. For about two hours, non-stop. Ados even woke up and scratched.

Eventually we lit the petrol bomb and saw big welts all over our bodies. Then the culprits! An army of little and large, fat, full-bodied, blood-full lice! They crawled up the walls and dropped off the sacking hanging on the roof. A plague of them!

We fled outside. I stripped off and washed myself under the village tap at midnight. Then we climbed, would you believe, onto the roof of an old broken shack and, at last, slept.

Srinigar: 1200 hours

We've turned away from the Alaknanda river valley and come through the most concentrated marijuana fields we have seen. The stuff is prolific!

Dick has hobbled along and I've taken a look at his toe: red, raw and swollen. There's obviously an ingrown nail. And incidentally, what a smell! It's turned into a dirty big problem. I've cut him a walking stick.

Dugadda: 1930 hours

Our heavy host is drunk. And very loud. He has a few English phrases which roar out of him. He tells us not to be afraid, we are safe here, he will look after us. These Indians have an odd way of being interested in us foreigners. Their attitude changes from place to place – one moment they crowd in on us (though we're never touched, except by the children who try pushing one another on to us then run off like blazes). Or else they affect complete disinterest, like here, pretending not to take any notice, but fill the chai shop in any case. Ados says this is purely coincidental. That the people around here are genuinely not interested in us. We are not that interesting.

I don't agree. We've had people practically wetting themselves to entertain or look after us. Or just to see what we're writing.

Day 63:
Tehri: 1600 hours

This is a sprawling town. About the biggest since Kathmandu, with a jam-packed bazaar. We find a real hotel, with real mattresses, real electricity and privacy. Despite Dick's toe we made good progress, travelling through low altitude hills and valleys. The path was zigzaggy and short cuts were satisfyingly plentiful.

. . . . . .

I've overdone the effort today. The last couple of miles were endless. My toe is tightly strapped and if I bump it as I did on the chair this evening it's excruciating. I crumpled up and nearly burst out crying.

Day 64:
Chham

Talk about the tail wagging the dog – my toenail threatens to drive me to surrender as it digs itself deeper and deeper into my toe. It's actually quite dramatic but I tell myself I'm a glutton for punishment, I'm a masochist, I enjoy the pain as much as the highs of pleasure, so, of course, I can walk on!

Then I'm hit by doubt and cannot bear to think I have got this far and may not make it. Nor do I want to be responsible for messing up my brother's attempt.

We contemplate the option – do we split up? Do I have a quick bit of surgery? Should Ados go on and I chase after him when the toe is repaired? If I can't keep up, can I skip around the south of the mountains?

Day 65:
Barhmakhali

We're in good spirits and sing a big chunk of our version of 'Ten Green Bottles' – from 'A hundred days of running waiting to be run,' down to fifty-five. At the end of each verse we chant the names of our overnight stops. The full recital would require five-and-a-half hours for its 5600 lines as well as a good memory! We sang for two hours and got half-way through.

Day 66:
Yamuna River Valley

Yesterday was one of our Top Five Hardest efforts: thirty-two miles with 5500 feet of climbing in eleven and a quarter hours between 0520 and 2045 hours. Must take my hat off to Dick who did it with his walking stick and utter concentration. His improvised technique kept his toe off the ground. But our effort took us beyond village life and we slept in a deserted house. Our second night without a meal.

Sonali: 1900 hours

Ados is excited: we've passed Barkot ahead of schedule. But for me this has been a diabolical day. A real grotty bore. I was head down all the way, struggling along and groaning to myself. In contrast, Ados has been wittering away continually.

We arrived at this chai house in heavy rain and now it's falling rattle-rattle on the roof and pitter-patter in the puddles. We've got stale bread buns and eggs for supper.

Ados says we've completed 499 hours and 55 minutes of actual travelling time. A more satisfactory statistic is that we have done two-thirds of our century.

When walking my thoughts are centred on my toe and I was concentrating so hard I failed to appreciate we'd actually crossed the Ganges valley yesterday.

Day 67:
Mori

A good stint before brunch today – fifteen miles. And we can actually see all the way to the finish! My pulse rate is sixty, Dick's sixty-six – not bad after such strenuous exercise.

Tiuni:

We've driven ourselves into the ground again – this time eleven hours forty minutes for thirty-two miles – our longest stint since before Kathmandu. My toe is behaving itself provided I don't stub it. Ados says I look like a crab, treading as I must on the outside of my foot. And now that's bruised! Poor me!

The weather brought the only excitement – a rush of black clouds, a screaming wind, frenetic lightning, bomb-blast thunder and a phenomenal ten-minute hail-storm. We huddled under a rocky overhang and watched the electric ice-show.

Day 68:
Arakot: 1000 hours

We are advancing due north now, up a moderately large river valley towards Rohru. And then we turn west over to Manali. For many days the country has been half-terraced, half-covered by tall hollow fir forest. The coarse dark green slopes have turned into verdant fields of grass – as though the mountainside were lawn. Not unlike the Lakes but bigger!

The people here seem less sophisticated. Perhaps its because we've left the pilgrim paths. More wear rags. More stand blankly and stare. The houses are small two-storey affairs with outsize slate roofs to cover the verandah round the house.

Not only the vegetation and houses have changed. The region we've entered is Himachal Pradesh and our first impressions are that it is more rural, less developed than Uttar Pradesh. Which means it is probably more touristy!

Day 69:
Rohru

Dear Steve,
Today is Day 69. We are reaching a big landmark of seventy-five days, three quarters of the traverse! This will mark the end of another section of our odyssey – our travels through the Indian foothills. We are really counting the days now.

Songri: 1330 hours
(top of 9000 foot pass)

From here, the country looks prosperous, the people and houses colourful. In fact, everything looks a little rosier. I produced a superbly normal stool this morning with only a small squidge of muck afterwards.

My toe is also holding together and after our night of luxury in the Kanchan Hotel (80 rupees – that's £5 for two) even my muscles have loosened up.

Beolthal: 1915 hours

Went for a short cut today that didn't come off. Ended up having to follow a water pipe just to get us somewhere. It took us to a lovely old world village with ornate wooden houses and visible women! And cattle living in the village square. But what a waste of time!

Locals, not too keen to offer us sleeping room, suggested a hotel in the next village but we haven't got there. Now dusk and we've decided to bed down on a high exposed turret that is a windy platform for separating wheat and chaff.

Day 70:
Majot: 0800 hours

We were worried about being mugged last night because five men had watched us bedding down. We awoke to shouting and were surrounded. The men had re-turned – with a pile of hot rice and sauce and two enormous piping hot chapatis.

We gulped this lot down, making grateful noises. I feel ashamed to have thought the locals would be aggressive. We've had nothing but kindness and curiosity.

My toe is a big brake on the end of my foot. It's not good today and I'm treading slowly, much to my brother's irritation. He's itching to get a move on. Going down hill I've got to be specially careful not to jam the toe against the shoe. Ados jigs about and dances down.

Koil: 1030 hours
(on the Sutlej river)

We bashed down a good path in a steep valley in the direction of the Sutlej River, then on to the even surface of a disused irrigation channel that suddenly breaks its course and dumps us into the main valley.

Dick reminds me that, before we set out, it was said that all I needed to keep me content was a cup of tea and a newspaper. We reached a chai house and found yesterday's English newspaper being used for wrapping. Mmmmm. Mango and Maggie Thatcher's election for breakfast!

Baghiphul: 1830 hours

We crossed the Sutlej River, one of the big rivers, on a workman's cradle slung below a single hawser and propelled by a man on the far side pulling a rope. It was a cheap (one rupee), novel and fairly dodgy journey, for our feet dangled thirty feet above the swirling waters of a very wide torrent. Looking up you have this dramatic view of the slopes and above them the snow peaks.

This is a distinctly different zone of the Indian Himalayas, resembling the Nepalese terraces around Taplejung or Jubing. Unterraced areas are few and far between because every slope that can be traversed is harnessed. It's actually geography text book stuff and we're back on the 'ethnic' trail. The women, for instance, wear distinctive clothes, headscarves and pantaloons. They're all into bright colours, strong blues and pinks and floral patterns.

Bashleo Pass

The lure of this pass has dragged us here. Tomorrow we'll be up and over it and making for Manali.

I've lost my walking stick! In the excitement of our basket crossing I left it on the other side of the Sutlej. Can't say I'm too bothered though – my toe is bleeding quite freely and I think the rottenness has escaped. Relief, I hope, has set in. Ados has gone to bed. Claiming he was exhausted. It's not surprising, the way he's been pushing us. Or maybe my moaning has got him down.

Day 71:
Sarahan:
(7500 feet)

A beautiful climb before breakfast! We have come up from the rocky, noisy gorge along a steep track past boisterous waterfalls, country cottages and small wheat terraces set among leafy trees.

The valley, at first, was so narrow and deep the sun couldn't find a way into it. A steep zigzag took us to the top and yet another panorama – sixty miles of view over town and hilltop to the snow line.

Half a kilometre out of town we stop at this Public Works Department Resthouse. (It sounds dreadfully unromantic!) And sit in armchairs drinking tea on the verandah. This is what it must have been like in Raj time: the tinkle of teacup and spoon, the idling in chairs and the swept verandah with its wide view across the flower beds and clipped grass down to the village and the hills beyond. The colonial conversation might have faded away but the other sounds are still here – the birdsong, the waterfall making music in the distance, the bullock-man calling from the fields and the servants of Sarahan rattling the saucers ever so slightly and saying 'sahib'.

Breakfast comes perfectly served. On decent china for a change. And tea from a china pot. Dick still has to go and spoil it by eating out of the serving dish.

Banjar: 2000 hours

Up the 10,000-foot Bashleo Pass and down! We can call it a snow crossing. At least we found a snow patch and threw some obligatory snowballs. Now we're at our second government Resthouse of the day. Another grand place but they've put us in a back room. Even so, it has an en suite bathroom and I'll certainly exploit that!

Ados and I have come a long way. During the early days of our journey I was acutely aware of being a foreigner in an alien environment and used to dream of England. Now I no longer feel a foreigner here. It's hard to explain, but I feel at home.

20

The Rohtang La

OUT OF Aut, we headed due north up the wide Kulu Valley surrounded by subdued hills which reminded us of our Lake District. But that was short-lived. We came across road signs and billboards heralding lots of agricultural and horticultural projects, fruit-canning factories, electricity sub-stations, educational establishments and transport centres. We saw tractors, farm machinery and orchards; dead cars, smoking buses, concrete blocks and ribbon development. International aid and funding groups were well represented in the small print on the signboards.

The Himalayan Hotel in Buntar was run by a most courteous Sikh who offered us the best room in the house and an instant omelette as our hors d'oeuvre. Things brightened even more when we discovered that the meagre kitchen had the capacity to make toast! We were settling down to a final cup of after-dinner tea when the manager entered looking concerned. He was followed by five soldiers.

'Papers,' ordered the captain.

'Eh?' I replied in Cumbrian. I wasn't too sure what was happening.

'Do you want to see our passports?' said Ados.

'Yes. What have you got in that bag?' The captain pointed at our rucksack. We were treated to a full search of our belongings and our passports were perused with great interest but not much understanding. My name they gleaned from the front of the passport to be 'Liverpool'. We passed inspection and the soldiers immediately offered to buy our camera and running shoes. They left when we said no. The manager explained that they were looking for two Nepalese and that our entries in the hotel register had mentioned that we came from Nepal.

The next day we made our way up the valley, slowly gaining altitude to 5000 feet. We were climbing back into cooler country with pine forests coating the valley sides. Ahead, the snowy peaks north of Manali gradually grew higher and more distinct. By 5.30 in the afternoon, we reached the little village of Kalath only five miles south of Manali.

Although keen to reach Manali and our next equipment dump, we decided to stop in Kalath for the night so that we wouldn't by any chance have to stay in Manali for two nights. That would have spoiled a record we were building. Ever since Arughat Bazar, the scene of Adrian's illness, we had spent forty-six nights in different villages and were reluctant to spend two nights in one place.

We had rather expected to find reasonable accommodation here as the village is known for its hot springs and might be expected to have some tourist trade. We were sadly disappointed and resigned ourselves to a ramshackle dwelling where we were conducted to an upstairs room. There had once been glass in the window frame but no longer. We unpacked a few things to show that we did mean to stay the night. A small group of children watched us while the occupants of the next room wandered in and out. I really was not sure whether we had a room or a corridor.

Adrian: While Dick went downstairs with his diary and to check out his feet and then find out how dinner was progressing, I dragged myself slowly over to the cloud of steam that marked the hot spring. The pool was almost as derelict as the village, surrounded by pieces of rubbish and a large oil drum. Draped over the drum were a few pieces of clothing belonging to the several young men who sat beneath the fountain of water issuing from the spring. Not being certain how hot the water was, I stepped in cautiously. It was marvellous. My last dip had been way back in central Nepal at the hot springs of Tatopani.

Now at last I could lie back and relax. The locals were polite and indicated that I could sit anywhere I liked. But I was happy where I was. Except my trump card was missing. I stood up and fetched from my pile of dirty clothes a newspaper scrounged from the tea house. I returned to the centre of the pool, lay back in the water to luxuriate in the soggy news. Unfortunately, it was so parochial it went right over my head.

Richard: We left Kalath the following morning in time to arrive in Manali at 9 am and we went up the main street as the town was opening for business. There was a bazaar, today's newspapers, European goods, tourist stalls, a police box in the road, proper cafes and a tourist office, all the trappings of a real town. We wound through the town to John Banon's Hotel which was our contact point.

Weeks ago, John Banon was just a name in our address list, and the destination of a brown hold-all sent there from Delhi. But that morning, John Banon was splendidly flesh and blood. He welcomed us profusely and did the very best thing he could, which was to lead us straight to his great British Breakfast with proper tea, sausages and toast and marmalade.

We spent the morning around the breakfast table, deciding to get a quick start the next day. The next section was north over the Himalayas to the Tibetan plateau and then south again to Srinigar in Kashmir. This had barely entered our calculations until then. Suddenly it was there to be tackled.

We went through the equipment in the rucksacks and the brown bag, and saw that we had to buy gloves and another balaclava helmet. The next job was to study the maps, decide our route and get as much information as possible on the conditions ahead. I began to worry when the local news informed us there was a heavy snow fall and that people had not yet started to venture into the area after the winter.

The Tibetan Plateau stretches north from the Great Himalayas which form the southern rampart, and is crossed with mountain ranges. Here are some of the highest peaks in the world; among them lie barren plains and deserts forming an inhospitable wilderness. Because of the hostile climate at these altitudes, there was little incentive for people to settle. We would find only hardy yak herders and Buddhist monks in their isolated monasteries.

The locals produced their usual warnings and advised us to 'carry all the food you will need, check your tents and take a good guide'. We sat down and wrote some necessary letters. We told the folks back home that, although the trail news was bad, we were setting out, as agreed, to go north of the Himalayan chain, aiming for Ladakh. We estimated that at midday on the one hundredth day, we'd be somewhere on the road from Leh to Srinigar. That, we decided, was where we would stop. Yes. STOP. And climb down from the Himalayas. One hundred days was going to be enough for us. Rawalpindi was beyond our sights and who knew how long it would take us to reach there if we decided to go on?

Adrian: The next morning came filtering through my senses, but, before it dawned, I didn't want to know where I was; it was bound to be somewhere uncomfortable. After a minute or so, I squinted and found myself in my comfortable Manali bed. I indulged in the thought that I would soon be home: a hundred days minus seventy-four: only twenty-six days to go. Less than a month! And not much more than three weeks. But in that time we had to go to Leh.

'That's one tough trip,' as Karen would say. I wished she were with me, then a question mark started flashing like a light bulb. Leh? Why were we going to Leh anyway? If we stuck close to the northern flank of the Great Himalayas we could fight our way across to Padum, and then to Kargil, the north-westerly point of India, which surely – it had to be! – yes, it was! – would be a much better target for a traverse than this place Leh. Not only would we stay closer to the ridge line, but it would save us several days – days in which we could get to . . . Srinigar? 'We really could,' I thought. 'I think I've blown this wide open,' I said to myself. 'Dick! Dick! Come here!'

Richard: Ados' expression had 'run, brother, run!' written all over it. And his excited explanations animated the possibilities with all sorts of hope. We sat with the map which was illuminated by a route that, running south of Leh, could get us into Srinigar with six days to spare. That would give us enough time to get across the border into Pakistan and run into Rawalpindi on the hundredth day. We couldn't believe it! So we checked again, using string to measure the distances. Arithmetically the answer was easy. Assuming we could cover twenty-three miles a day, the end we had started with was suddenly in sight! For the first time in ages my pulse rate accelerated on pure excitement. As for Ados, he was ready to sprint the streets of Manali shouting 'Eureka!'

We had breakfast and worked out a plan of action. One snag was that our couriers had left the day before with out-of-date news! But John Banon pointed us towards the telegraph office. We drafted telegrams to Air India, Mountain Travel, and wrote fresh letters to IT and the family. In our rearrangement rush, Ados had a frustrating trip to Manali post office which kept him nearly one-and-a-half hours. For a so-called non-worrier, his big worry was whether the mail would get through and it was a fear I shared. A local tailor came up trumps with a new set of cotton tunics to replace our tattered Kathmandu originals, and we ended a hectic morning with a seventy-fifth day, 1500-mile celebration lunch. Pleasantly stunned by our change of plan, we collected up our things, left our hold-all stuffed with smelly gear for John to send on, and slipped quietly into our last twenty-five day stride.

By the following day we had climbed out of the north end of the Kulu valley to the slopes of the Rohtang pass and into the snow. On the way up we had a chai stop at Mahi at 11,000 feet which caters for the Indian tourists. Here well-fed, well-dressed Indians venture a few feet into the snow and throw snowballs. But we had to plough on.

Once again the altitude and the cold impressed us with the hard facts of travelling. At the top of the pass, we had reached 13,500 feet and it was going to be many days before we returned to less than 10,000 feet.

Beyond the summit, through the veil of mist, we saw mountains marching off into the clouds. Below us lay the cold white and grey of a valley. In the pale light, a river glinted like steel as it wound through snowbanks and rocks in the valley floor. As hard as we looked, we saw no welcoming wisps of smoke or twinkling fires. We had left the little villages, the yellow terraces and the green pine forests of the southern slopes for the shivering cold ahead. In no mood to spend time on the snowy wastes of Rohtang, we strode on as the gradient turned downwards. The snow was firm and we could glissade the steep bits and perform a sliding, skating motion over the flatter snowfields. No path guided us down into the 'Valley of the Gods' where, although habitation was sparse, we knew there should be a settlement a little way along the valley.

As we lost height we angled west on the slopes. This led us to the banks of a roaring torrent fed from the melting snows above. These streams are often quoted as the most dangerous part of a trip in mountain areas and we knew from our own experience that we must find the best crossing point possible. It took us half an hour clambering up and down the steep gorge to find a huge jumble of boulders within which the stream hissed and poured. Adrian went first, clambering across two huge rocks and then balanced atop the last before launching himself in a horrifyingly casual leap fifteen feet above the roaring water. I, too scared to jump, waded waist-deep towards the other side, afraid that any second I'd be swept away. Water hammered against my chest but it was only a minute across and I landed on the other side safe but numb.

I was overjoyed when we saw a simple building. We arrived to hear an old paraffin pressure stove sizzling in the darkness at the back of an unlit room. Following our own invitation yet again, we slipped inside and settled down for the night. One day out of Manali, we had climbed over the Rohtang La. I was already knackered, and had lost my enthusiasm. My guts were far from well and the night before I didn't know whether I was coming or going. In addition, I kept bumping my very sore big toe and a sharply painful little toe against the rocks as I bumbled blindly around the hillside without my contacts.

Inside, I kept getting cramp and ended up jammed in a sitting position on the dirty window sill and slept there. At that moment I didn't want much out of life – just a sit-down loo, an electric light and a book to read. I couldn't even anaesthetise myself in my diary because I had no light.

In some desperation, I had started taking Streptotriad to tame the constant bug and Ados was also taking the treatment. Otherwise, he was streets stronger than me. So much so, that I was even tempted, coming over the pass, to give him something extra to carry. It was no way to tackle the Tibetan plateau.

Adrian: I had been quite worried about Dick making such hard work of the pass. But I was happier about his lack of grumbles and this was uncharitable because he was obviously just worn out from fighting his poisoned system. His first treatment hadn't helped and he was sleeping so badly his body just didn't have a chance. I, on the other hand, was feeling well, despite the old tum. Even my legs were losing their ache. I invariably felt so much better as we climbed up high to the cold and the snow. Blizzards and ice I could cope with, village kids and flies buzzing me in the heat I could not. Perhaps Dick was right, it was all in the mind. In a draughty hut in the Himalayas I was in my element. We had taken on the simple challenge of Rohtang and passed the test. I was confident and happy. Ready for whatever challenges were in store. And the only big one I could see remaining was to surmount the Shingo La and get onto the Tibetan Plateau.

21

Meeting Place

THE MOST immediate challenge, apart from just putting one foot in front of the other, lay a few miles ahead. It was the competition we'd been following ever since we'd started from Darjeeling and would now catch up.

On Day 77 we reached Kyelang, the capital of the Lahoul and Spiti District of Himachal Pradesh. We had travelled down a splendid valley for twenty miles from Rohtang La almost to the junction of the Chandra and Bhaga rivers. It was so good that instead of my customary moans, I was moved to wax lyrical about 'the most magnificently serrated high mountain ridge of this traverse'.

In Kyelang, we contemplated two days on the snows of Shingo La and for some reason were so awe-struck in anticipation that we decided to break one of our golden rules – we would carry food with us. We stocked up our bellies with a massive meal of a huge plate of rice, four chapatis, lentil soup called dahl, and vegetables curry then we each ate two chapatis to tide us over in case we found nothing else.

We were, however, over-confident that evening about finding overnight accommodation. Expecting it to be easy, we left Kyelang after six, got caught in the rain, eventually found a solitary house two hours after dark but no amount of hailing and sweet talk directed at a head that appeared at an upstairs window had any effect. We were forced to move on, bemoaning the failure of the Crane charm. Unable to find another house, we laid our Gore-Tex jackets, trousers and our sleeping bags on the stony track for a sub-zero night out.

Early next morning we hit Gemur, a nondescript village halfway up the mountainside, and had just sighed ourselves down in a dirty smoky chai house when a head of spiky hair materialised in front of us.

'Pam!' we shouted. And Pam shrieked. We hadn't seen her since our very first visit to Kathmandu and the meeting called for hugs and kisses. She, of course, was Pamela Tubby who, with Elaine Brooks, had set out on the British Women's Trans-Himalayan Expedition from Sikkim in January. We had had snippets of their progress.

She told us they were having money problems because they were paying 'extortionate' porter wages of fifty rupees a day. It brought home to me how fortunate we were. Because there were only two of us with no porters nor guides, we could, in Nepal or India, afford anything we wanted without asking the price. Adrian's £5000 investment in the expedition had turned out to be quite sufficient. We were also

94

prepared to agree that it was money well spent. Indeed we had already raised more than that amount of money for Intermediate Technology to use on its charitable work throughout the world.

Our meeting with Pam obviously propelled her team into fresh decisions for, after leaving us for fifteen minutes, they came rushing back to say that they were ditching their porters, most of their food and would go lightweight with twenty to thirty pound packs. Because they were an official expedition, the liaison woman would naturally carry on too, and they'd pick up a guide for the Shingo La. Meantime they had a bit of mad sorting out to do. I gleefully pictured the team in the middle of Gemur, throwing clothes, food, medicines and papers all over the place!

I confided to my diary that 'this was a last ditch attempt to beat us on the traverse. They only have to get ninety kilometres to Padum, then catch a bus to Kargil and Leh to finish. We still have 600 kilometres to go on foot!'

In retrospect, it was petty to be worried that our friendly rivals might claim the first British traverse from their finishing point in Northern India. However, I couldn't help recalling an adage that I had come to trust: 'The promise is remembered, the conditions forgotten.' I knew that the media and the history books would not remember where or when either team started, how the traverses had been carried out or where we had ended. They would care only about the first claim. I felt that we had to make it first – and catch the headlines first.

Ados wasn't going to let such considerations bother him. Fate and the future would sort things out with a bit of effort from us. But I could see the fear sitting on my damn mind for days. As if I didn't have enough to worry me.

22

Towards the Plateau

Adrian: Dawn turned the night sky pale in the East and the small sickle moon faded with the stars. The wind knifed through my sleeping bag stabbing me awake. I lay in my sleeping bag with the hood of my duvet drawn close around my face. As long as I remained still there was a pocket of warm air about me but as I raised my head, fingers of freezing air crawled down my neck. We were in a rock and snow valley at 12,500 feet with the wind blowing dry snow through the stones of our low windbreak and the temperature way below zero.

It was our second bivvy in a row. The carpet of moss and grasses, running shoes and Gore-Tex that we had laid to keep out the cold was now strewn about from our midnight struggles to ease the ache of cold bones against hard ground. Inches from my head were the charred remains of the tiny fire that had flickered in the thin air as we tried to warm our hands and toes.

Richard: Looking across at Ados I saw only his nose, smeared with soot, peeping from under the drawstrings and balaclava. As I began the first moves of the new day, my brother groaned and rolled over. I wriggled over to the little crevice in a stone where my contact lenses lay, and with numb fingers slipped them from the scrap of Michèle's handkerchief into my mouth. Then with great care I put them, cleaned and warmed, to my eyes. The world looked even colder in the hard angularity of perfect sight. 'Pity I don't have good eyes,' I thought, 'my only imperfection.' Then as an afterthought 'That and my idea of fun'. Little brother would have said it had he been awake.

Adrian: Dick was sitting half upright when I opened my eyes. We got moving at once.

I hoped that Dick had got a little sleep. We were nearing the pass now and the problems would be formidable. Since leaving Manali, Dick had at last begun to share my feeling that the end was in sight.

Getting out of our bags was like jumping into the cold sea on the West Cumbrian coast, only there we weren't fully dressed! Putting on our shoes and packing away the sleeping bags took only a moment and, by the time I had remembered the camera, there was no bivouac site to photograph! I snapped the circle of rocks anyway, and set off. We kept going until the sun rose over the eastern wall of the valley and its warmth crept down to us over the snowy slopes. Then we stopped and the duvets came off. We packed them away and tore off half a cold chapati to divide for breakfast.

Dick munched each morsel carefully as I studied the maps. They were three scraps cut from large maps which we could combine to give a useful picture of the terrain. In this wild country, we had to choose the correct side valley from dead reckoning of distance, and I combed the maps for more clues.

There was a river between us and our valley's entrance and, as we approached it, we searched for a crossing point. The river was shallow but wide, and we didn't relish the thought of that cold water. Hoping for an alternative, I stared up the valley to where a sweep of snow crossed unbroken from peak to peak. There was our answer. A snowslope so large that the water had not breached it and instead flowed through a tunnel beneath. We had seen several of these snow bridges lower in the valley, delicate spans that one would not dare tread, but here, where it was higher and colder, the snow was thick and firm and took us across.

After scrambling up the steep side of the main valley we entered the narrow mouth of our side valley. We followed the stream along the foot of the confining mountains until the snow cover increased and the stream was lost for long periods below the white blanket. We climbed and climbed, the mountains unfolding below in all their intricacy. We stopped for rests and a salt biscuit, washed down with meltwater full of icy granules, but it was too cold to stay still for long.

Then the weather closed in. There were dark clouds in the north and the mist swirled in on the nearby peaks. The valley seemed to go downhill but we were always climbing uphill when we looked over our shoulders. Fear of the worsening weather weighed on me. Then it began to snow, lightly at first, turning to a white-out as the clouds closed in. We didn't want to bivouac here at 18,000 feet and we couldn't see where we were going. Our maps weren't any help either. We must have been pretty stretched, as in my diary I wrote: 'I only continued because I knew I could retrace my footsteps to safety.'

We crunched on to find, at last, the summit cairn and an array of prayer flags. The veil of snow on the near slopes ebbed and flowed across us. We were unable to judge how steep the slopes were in the strange light. Consequently we slithered down them, negotiating ice cliffs, and finally stopped on the rough surface of avalanche debris.

The snow stopped and we went on, to the wide, snowless gravel beds of the Zanskar valley. It was late afternoon. We stopped again and ate the remaining scraps of soggy chapati. Our morale had risen considerably with the crossing of Shingo La. We were entering, for the first time, the state of Jammu and Kashmir, we had escaped from the snows and our descent had been fast and fun. The crossing had also taken us over the line of the Great Himalayas – we were north of them now – into central Asia.

As evening advanced we became increasingly aware of the desolation of the Tibetan plateau. We approached several huts that turned out to be nothing but big boulders. Then, in the distance, several dark images turned out to be a yak nomads camp. We stopped a few yards short of the encampment.

97

Richard: I stepped forward over the low stone barriers to the centre of the camp. A couple of children had seen us and dashed off to spread the news.

A short distance across the rocks a heavily fur-clad man was tending two shaggy yaks, their white horns almost luminous against the black background of their coats. The children returned with an older woman who may have been their mother or their sister. I smiled and held my hands together in greeting. Ados said something like 'Goo'daaay', assuring me that it meant 'hello' in Tibetan. The woman's chubby face lit up. She giggled and the children nestled in closer behind her. I shivered demonstratively and rubbed my arms to show how cold I felt. It was no act. We both rubbed our stomachs and gestured to our mouths. After a furious burst of chatter, the little girl ran off, to return a few moments later with a bowl of dry tsampa.

I wondered if this was all – just a bowl of barley flour in the cold?

'Chai, chai,' said Ados.

'La, la,' said the little boy, wagging his finger in schoolmasterly fashion without getting his point across. It seemed clear that negotiating was going to be difficult.

A young man and another older woman appeared next from the low entrance of the nearest tent. The boy retreated to his elders' ragged coat tails. We repeated our greetings and Ados followed quickly with his practised rendering of 'Chai? chai?' Eventually another child appeared with a brass cup of slimy white liquid and handed it to us. With my audience captivated, I mixed the contents into the tsampa and tried the paste. The sensation of food was superb. I analysed the taste: it was like sour yoghurt mixed with stale digestive biscuits.

I fixed my eyes on the young man, put my hands to my head and feigned sleep. The man didn't seem to understand. I tried again, enlisting Ados to reinforce my mime. The little boy's finger wagged again from behind his protective elder. Finally, the young man's fixed expression broke: he turned and beckoned us to follow. We were led behind the near tent to another tent attached to it. We followed our host through the narrow tent flap. Two clods of earth were pulled from the edges of the tent for us to squat on while the young man scraped together twigs from the floor and prepared a fire. The little group which huddled in the door dispersed on errands. One returned with a lighted stick for the fire, one with our abandoned tsampa and a cup of yoghurt, and a third struggled through the door with tea-making kit: balls of dirty butter, a pot, stirring spoon, green and brown leaves and big cubes of salt.

Once the fire was flickering between the three stones that would support the pot, the young man left with two of his helpers while the girl busied herself with tea making. We relaxed, settled ourselves against our soft rucksacks and watched her work.

I assumed the group we'd come across to be Zanskari nomads, Mongoloid in appearance, their faces tanned a deep brown. They all wore thick ragged yak-wool tops and trousers, yak skin shawls, boots and Tibetan head gear – round topi with upturned ears. Just as evocative as their appearance was their smell: that distinctive smell of people who never wash, mixed with yak. Their lives depend on the yak: milk, butter, meat, fur, skins, even to the extent that they have to burn dried yak dung as fuel because wood is so scarce.

The tent was a heavy wool blanket supported by two poles, stretched to meet the low stone walls that formed its base. Beneath it the girl added yak dung and heather to the fire. We watched as the tea and salt and butter were churned together in the pot. Ados used the empty yoghurt cup while I had our plastic water container. The tea was perfect, and we persuaded her to start immediately on a second potful.

After our meal we unfurled our sleeping bags and laid them on thick mats covering the dusty ground. Wet shoes and socks came off and we toasted our feet near the fire. Aware that the hearth is sacred and should not be violated by steaming socks, we spread them at the back of the tent. I tried to put down some thoughts in my diary about Shingo La but had to stop because the flickering fire was useless as a light. In the yellow glow I saw Ados snuggle into his sleeping bag. As I followed suit I couldn't help thinking: how do these people survive up here?

The young man then returned to our tent to drink tea with us and we tried to explain where we had come from and who we were. He left smiling, and more yoghurt was brought in by a pretty, wide-eyed girl. Then we were interrupted by a shuffling at the door. The flap was opened and two yak calves crept into the tent. Tethered to the rocks, they stayed with us, shuffling and sniffing and eyeing their strange bedfellows.

We nudged some more lumps of dry dung onto the smouldering fire and lay back. The yak camp was a luxury, a delight. I went out one last time to the wind and sleet just to see how nice it was to come in again. We slept soundly that night, our heads nestling happily into pillows of rock.

Morning arrived via the smoke hole in the tent. A girl squatted beside the fire coaxing the embers to life. Behind her the young yaks were stepping around among the cooking implements. As the girl reached for a bowl or a flask she would push the animals off and then rub the mud from the vessel with one of her skirts. Tea was already made before I woke Ados. 'Not your normal bed tea,' I said, as he fixed me with a bleary eye.

I took my bowl of tsampa and tea outside where the sun's rays were warming the breeze. The scenery was magnificent. The horizon rose from sheer valley walls to jagged heights. Behind me the blue river narrowed to a pinpoint. In front of me, across an ocean of boulders, was the prow of a huge ship, its orange sides flecked with white streaks of foam. In the fading light of the evening before, the same vast wall had swept upwards like some giant fish fin. Now it loomed as formidable as a battleship.

The yak herd was being led from their tethering places in the lee of the tents to eke out another day on the sparse grass among the stones. A group of herd boys whistled and jostled the animals, aware I was watching their performance. The pretty young girl who had made our tea last night was walking slowly up from the river. On her back she carried a large wicker basket partly filled with yak-dung fuel. When she stopped close to us, her younger brother ran up waving his finger at us again and shouting 'La, la', which one could interpret as 'lay off my sister'. She certainly seemed fascinated by us or it might have been our bright bulbous blue duvets and shiny windproof trousers. She herself was close to Himalayan haute couture, with a long-haired animal skin covering her shoulders and a thick black robe belted with a white wool string. In addition, she wore a number of bracelets.

A much older woman, wearing a turquoise and coral headpiece, seemed less interested in the two handsome strangers. She followed the trail of the yaks, picking up cakes of dung and tossing them carefully over her shoulder into the basket on her back. Her load looked heavy, making her bend.

We sought out the young man, our host, and thanked him profusely for his hospitality. He came out of the tent and smiled an acknowledgement, then waved us off down the valley towards the nearest village of Kurgiakh with directions for our journey, none of which we could understand. With a feeling of sadness, I hitched up my gear and set off after Ados, who was already making tracks.

Adrian: Once out of sight of the camp, just one hummock away, we were alone again. We descended the valley towards a track we could see across the land ahead. It grew from an inconsistent smudge on the gravel banks to a clear line across flat sandy areas of meagre grass that we could follow. After three hours we came upon a shoulder where the trail curved around its side and on the skyline stood the unmistakable shape of a chorten. Behind it, like a bride's train, was a low mani wall containing thousands of flat stones on which travellers over the centuries had laboriously carved the mantra 'Om Mani Padme Hum' in order to ensure good favour for their journeys.

At the shoulder we could look down on a small vale tinged with the green of a sparse crop of barley and scattered with great orange boulders. The crop was the indication that we were close to a village, and on rounding the shoulder we saw a cluster of flat houses set into the rising land at the back of the vale. We immediately felt hungry again!

The village seemed deserted save for an old man who was sitting on a wall watching the barley grow. We explained our needs in the universal sign language. He was happy to humour us and led us to a little patio in front of a house. A large grey rug was laid on the dry mud surface and we slipped off our rucksacks and sat, propping ourselves against the wall. Because of the aches in our legs we could only sit cross-legged with difficulty, so we used to make a beeline for places with something to lean against or seats to sit on. We also tried to beat each other to the best spot or be first to the post. But I wasn't content to sit there and went hunting for food. I stooped under the low door and into the dark. I had to stop a moment to accustom my glasses to the dark inside the house. Then I saw, hanging over the doorway, a charm made of strips of red and green cloth tied to the claws and head of a long dead eagle. I moved on, following the sound and smell of a room in use. Although this dwelling looked square from outside there appeared to be no pattern to the rooms. The ceilings were low, the rooms dark and filthy, covered in soot.

In the kitchen I found a man by the fire. He had odd pots and pans around him and in one corner lay a pile of blankets, on one of which was a hunk of meat. While he watched me, I inspected each vessel carefully and came up with a satisfactory supply: one large bag full of flour, a big urn of water, a tin box containing huge lumps of salt and the meat. The meat did not look at all appetising. With considerable difficulty, I tried to arrange for a meal of meat, but didn't get very far. So I asked him

Smiling Nepalese woman.

Ados tucking into his food in front of an audience. Chapati and curry.

Nepalese man.

Ados collecting glacier meltwater to drink.

Goods for sale or barter in a Nepalese haat bazaar.

A Tibetan yak nomad at 13,500 ft.

Ados beside an Intermediate Technology cooking stove. This one is 35% more efficient than the earlier type and also has a flue to extract smoke and fumes from the living area.

Dick tries to make chapati with flour given to us by some porters during a night in the open.

A Nepalese lady.

to make us tea. That done, I tried discussing the lunch menu again. I was getting frustrated. As had been the case throughout our trip, the words 'hurry! now! fast! five minutes!' just did not convey any meaning, let alone urgency. And, whatever Dick said, it was going to take me more than a hundred days to be cured of the habits of an impatient western executive! The man and I sipped our tea and I started again:

'Chapati,' I ventured.

'Chha,' he nodded. There is.

'Chapati,' I repeated, stabbing my chest with a finger.

'Hajur,' he smiled. Okay.

'Chapati, Bhok laagchha,' I tried in Nepali, rubbing my stomach.

'Hajur,' he nodded and smiled.

I rose, picked up a bowl, mixed some flour and water and returned to the fire. The message was understood, he took a large bowl and started the routine that I knew would lead to chapatis in an hour. Still the closest thing to an instant snack out here.

While the cooking got under way, I explored an adjacent room and returned with a butter ball and a pocketful of tsampa, just to keep us going until the chapatis arrived. Since I had already invested so much energy in this meal, I decided to reach for the sky.

'Sugar?' I asked. I could already imagine a thick, hot chapati running with butter and sprinkled thickly with sugar. 'Please, pretty please, sugar?' I repeated without much hope. But his eyes lit up.

'Chainna' (not here) he said and waved his hands around the room. Then he gestured beyond his house to the outside. 'Chha – there is,' he said.

I produced money and a friend was summoned. I was to be taken shopping. Through a maze of little rooms, I was led out into the glare. Across the village and into another warren. I stood fast, grasping the friend's hand while my eyes adjusted. In the dark room, several little bags, knotted at the top, lay on the floor. The friend carefully untied a knot and there lay the silver treasure of Kurgiakh! It was probably only three days since I last had sugar but this looked beautiful. It would surprise Dick! I splashed out and bought a handful costing a whole rupee, almost seven pence. I returned to Dick in high spirits to show off my treasure but he sounded ungrateful and I felt a bit cheesed off. I stormed off as far away as I could get from my brother, which was to the other side of the patio. I couldn't afford to miss those chapatis when they came.

Richard: I was not sure what had got into Ados, except that he was obviously frustrated by our slow progress. Maybe he was suffering from sugar withdrawal symptoms! I slipped inside the house to check on how long it would take to prepare the meat and have a search for any cooked scraps that Ados had missed. The local people always seemed to find it fun when we took the initiative and we had long since lost our inhibitions about other peoples' houses. I wondered where all the women were, perhaps out in the fields.

Meat was, indeed, a lost cause, but the chapatis were in full swing and a pile was building up on the edge of the hearth. I ducked out of the kitchen and returned to the patio to see that Ados had simmered down and was tucking into more tea and tsampa with a vigour that powdered his moustache and duvet with white flour.

For the simple reason that we both relied on each other so much, we could not afford the disruption of long disputes. Whether we were on course for a major bust-up at the end I could not tell, but for the moment we were back on course. That's the beauty of being brothers: it doesn't really matter how we feel because we're brothers whatever.

23

A Monastery

Richard: From Kurgiakh and Char we continued down gully and gorge and found Reru – a fascinating old town clinging to a crag in a lonely land. The town is a labyrinth of fortress-like white-walled dwellings with tiny windows. Their flat roofs are raised to a whole variety of levels, but the most interesting thing about the roofs were the women who sat on them, sewing and combing wool in the sun.

When we looked up at them, they burst into teasing laughter, their faces beautifully alive. They were all dressed in their yak wool but they were obviously sun worshippers as well, for they had bared their bosoms. They grew excited at having their photographs taken, jumping around and jabbering. After the hidden women of the Indian foothills, it was a delight to experience the uninhibited friendliness of the Tibetan women in these remote villages. Wrapped in layers of long black wool and yak skins with thick yak boots and elaborate head-dress, their ample figures were topped with shiny red moon faces. When you tried speaking to them they creased up in laughter, bouncing off one another. They hadn't, it seemed, a care in the world.

Adrian: We had been following the north-west porters' trade route down the valley for most of the afternoon and there seemed no end to it.

'This is getting ridiculous,' I thought.

Steep scree slopes of broken rock hung above cliffs that ran down sheer to the swirling grey waters of the river. Snow and ice festooned the crags above our path. Hidden away in sunless corners, other patches of ice were reminders of the winter that only one month ago had blanketed the whole land.

The track clung to the rock, winding up and down as it searched for a way out of the steep canyon. There was absolutely no question of crossing the river. There were no bridges and swimming the churning cold was unthinkable. This was the most starkly hostile and desolate country we had been in. Grey, cold and barren. All around us the rock and ice faces creaked and cracked like some monstrous animated sculpture.

In dwindling light we turned yet another twist of the gorge and suddenly came upon a low wall of carved mani stones and two leaning flag poles, their prayer fabric fluttering busily. Some way beyond stood a huge slab of rock on which was perched a cluster of buildings like a picture out of a fairy tale.

103

As we approached the foot of this pyramid, the track widened, then split into a sweep around the base of the rock and on down the valley. A steep path angled up the rock to the lowest point of the smooth walls that encircled the summit. A higher path led through a pair of open gates and past a low barred window where I half expected a guard to be sitting. We climbed beyond the gate to a higher gateway in the inner wall and up a short wide tunnel to a central courtyard.

The place was quiet. Eventually a young man appeared and walked up to us. His head was shaven and he was dressed in the long maroon coat of a Buddhist monk. He looked even too young to be a man. Maybe only fourteen. He smiled and giggled and then skipped about with glee in front of us. Our first questions he left unanswered as he touched and fingered our gear and then pointed up and down the valley, obviously curious about our route. We quickly got in our requests for tea and food. He whooped, heaven knows why, and then gave us his attention.

'Chia, Chia,' he laughed, mimicking our questions before answering them with a positive though incomprehensible flood of words. He directed us to the large porch of the tallest part of the building and, reassuring us with smiles and kind-sounding words, he skipped off. He was soon replaced by a tiny boy in layers of dirty grey cloth who stood at a distance and sucked on his sleeve while he watched us make ourselves comfortable. A long while went by. The little boy was uncommunicative. Tea was not forthcoming.

When the young monk returned he was carrying a candle and asked us to follow him. It transpired that we were to have a conducted tour of the Bardon Gompa, a monastery in the long process of renovation, in return for a small donation to the building and to our young guide. Rather run-down, it is not the most celebrated of monasteries but we were stuck with the tour.

From the outside, the gompa is a complex of white walls stacked together randomly like building bricks, on a rocky promontory. Inside, it is a maze of miniature doorways, tunnels, rooms and roofs all at different levels and most of them dark. The walls are built of bare cold rock, the floors are lumpy, uneven clay.

Dick parted with five rupees, and we set off in pursuit of our young guide who had disappeared through one of the low doors. We hoped it wouldn't take long. We had had a long hard day through fearsome country, and I could have done without trailing round seeing the sights. Dick, though, put on his I-am-keenly-interested-in-all-this-ethnicity look and hurried after the lad. I didn't mind fighting hard every inch of the way to get to Rawalpindi but it annoyed me to add even one extra step to our route. I already felt Dick was holding us up because of his lack of pace during the day and it was absurd that he should waste his energy on these extraneous activities. He had spent most of the last few days complaining about my photographs or his feet or his guts or me. The only smiles he had were reserved for the locals. I told him our venture had become of secondary importance to him. It wasn't so but I did want him to pull finger.

We climbed a dark stairway and emerged into a large room with great big windows lit with the last of the evening light. In the corner was a huge gong. With requisite ceremony the young monk took up two sticks and, bowing to his audience of two, began to play. When the tinny solo was finished he beat more sombre notes on the gong with a heavy cloth-coated hammer. As the last echoes faded, the young monk's reverent expression switched again to that of a giggly boy and he swept us out of a door up to a parapet overlooking the middle of the building.

'What an amazing place!' Dick whispered and my reply was typical.

'I think you're right but I'm in no mood to enjoy it now.'

'I really can't understand you,' he said, sounding wounded. 'You won't get another chance to see this sort of thing and it must be worth a few moments to look at.'

'Except that we are here to run the bloody Himalayas not to sightsee. It's no wonder things are tough if you want to study the culture, learn the language, check out the geology *and* run.'

'It wasn't me that got ill and had to stop for a whole day, was it? I've had bad guts and that swollen toe and have kept going all the time.'

'Well, it was hardly my fault if I was physically unable to go on.' I could feel the old argument coming on.

'It's all in the mind and you were too weak-minded to go on. I could hardly walk with my bad toe, back before Manali, and yet you were happy to let me keep going then,' Dick went on.

I was getting very sick of his continual harking back to my day of illness which stopped us completely in Nepal. Every time I commented on ways of speeding us up I would be met with the same line of attack.

'If it's all in the mind then why the hell do we ever stop? How come it's okay for your mind to be weak now?' I started to shout.

Dick smirked. 'You'll just have to accept the fact that the two of us have chosen to stop here tonight. It is fact.'

I could see that we were rapidly getting to conflicting basic philosophy, so I let the argument drop.

'Perhaps Dick has a point,' I thought. 'I don't often have the chance to stand and gawp at a gompa in the middle of nowhere.' I smiled. 'Let's go see the throne room.'

The monk took us down the windy stairs again, out to the courtyard and into the monastery's main chamber. From a library rack at the back of the room Dick picked up a package of paper held between two boards and tied up with a strip of cloth. The young monk watched as he undid the knotted cloth and lifted the board off the top. He turned several of the yellow sheets, crackling with age, and then carefully tied up the bundle again and replaced it in its place in the rack.

When would it next be untied? I wondered. I tried to imagine some long dead monk working at the script and wondered what it could mean.

'You realise what we have just seen? Something wonderful,' I said to my brother. He looked at me as though he wasn't altogether sure I was being serious.

Richard: Supper time in an almost defunct monastery. One monk in maroon robe and hat with turned up ears, one trainee, one little boy, one Zanskari traveller, and two Englishmen sit on rugs on the floor of a tiny smoke-filled room with one tiny window. It is dark outside and the wind howls. Light comes from a petrol wick lamp and the dung fire on which our guide cooks po-ba (tsampa balls in soup). Ados

105

was happy to lie back and enjoy the flickering fire. I however withdrew into my diary.

Adrian: That night we laid our bright blue sleeping bags and red jackets out on the entrance porch in front of the big doors of the library. From where I lay I could see ghostly creatures hidden in the shapes on the walls. It was weird. And to escape my imagination I looked out through the courtyard, past the silhouette of the monastery and up to the bright stars for some solid reassurance before falling into a deep contented sleep.

The next day we were on the path to Padum and I was trying to ask the way of the old Zanskari in Nepali. He did not take quickly to my disjointed phrasing. When I asked how far it was, he lifted his walking stick and used one finger to point to the finger that he had uncurled from his other gnarled hand. We figured he was saying one hour. One hour to Padum! We were nearly there!

Ever since Shingo La it had been the next big target. And now the regional headquarters of Zanskar was just around the corner.

The jumble of shapes at the top of the incline turned out to be houses. I urged Dick up the hill and we soon stood overlooking a rather sparse collection of houses and buildings. In the foreground a number of large houses stood well apart. They were painted in red, white and blue. Down to the right were the older, more closely packed houses of the original village. Beyond these, a flat plain, puffed with swirls of dust, stretched to the far-off ramparts of the next mountain range.

We approached the closest house but no answer came to our knocks and shouts. We tried the next, again silence. At one house we found a youth sitting on the step but he spoke only in negatives: no food, no bed, no people, no nothing. We should go to the village centre which seemed pretty lifeless.

In a little shop all boarded up and piled high with empty-looking packets and cardboard boxes, three men were squatting around a primus stove. A bed frame with a network of wire springs was the central piece of furniture and Dick dug himself a place to sit among the boxes. The men seemed unperturbed by our arrival and, yes, we could share their tea. The brew on the stove was almost ready and between their two cups, the pan, our water container and a tin can, all five of us were soon sipping and slurping.

One of the three men was dressed in European trousers and shirt with a couple of jackets around his shoulders for warmth. He said his name was Chhom Bel Bodh and he could speak some English. He told us he had only recently arrived in Padum from Kubi, south of the mountains. He came by way of a 23,000-foot pass and had suffered all manner of hardships during his journey, but had coped with them because he was a top class mountaineer.

'And what kind of equipment did you have?' I asked him.

'These very shoes,' he replied, pointing to his once-fashionable pair. 'And a scarf.' The shoes had gaping holes and I thought that for this guy to cross a 23,000-foot pass in spring, wearing ordinary shoes, he must have to be a very fine mountain man indeed. It was a doubtful claim but before I queried it I realised that it might not be too long before we would be back in London claiming to have run the Himalayas in running shoes!

Rice and dhal turned out to be a gourmet meal in comparison with the chapati and tsampa we'd been eating for so long. There wasn't anything else on offer here according to our friend who said Padum was a seasonal town. It was only just the end of a particularly hard winter and the town was starting to open up. Some of its 3000 residents went south in the winter and Chhom was the first of the summer residents to return.

He told us he had a hotel and this restaurant, and would be starting business in about a month. That's when the foreign trekkers would be coming in from the north and the passes would be open.

There was, we learned, a motorable track to Kargil, although it was only open for about two months in late summer. This year the road would be late opening due to the bad winter and might not yet be cleared of snow.

I asked Chhom where in the town I could go to buy supplies. He smiled and explained that although this was a trading town there was nothing to buy now. No supplies had come in since last year and those had either been sold or eaten over the winter. He said he was sharing his rice with us only because we were fellow mountaineers.

I looked around the shop. Chhom was right, there was nothing much left. Several pairs of black plimsoll shoes, four packets of biscuits in heavily waxed paper, some ballpens and some cigarettes in conical shaped packets. We devoured all four packets of biscuits but they were miserably stale.

As for the other trading stores, Chhom said today was the day before polling in the All-India elections and the local people were having a holiday. They were all inside because of the cold.

While Dick wrote his diary I went to forage around the village for food. Chhom was right, there was nothing happening. I did, however, rustle up one man who took me to his little shop and opened it for my benefit. I rummaged around in his cardboard boxes and containers and came up with two handfuls of boiled sweets and some antiseptic cream which had separated into its components after being so long in the tube. Each squeeze produced an oily perfume to rub on my chapped lips and weather-red cheeks. We gave it away later as we left town.

Richard: When Ados returned from his foray to the shops he found a sliver of soap in the dirt behind the cooking stove and dashed out to wash his hands. I couldn't be bothered. He came back bouncing through the gap in the boards covering the shop front and displaying his 'purfickly' clean hands.

Padum was at the junction of two routes, one going north to Leh or Lamayuru and the other west along the line of the Great Himalayas to Kargil. This we had decided was the quicker route but I asked Chhom what he thought.

'All is very difficult. But you are good mountaineers. There is still much snow. The rivers are very dangerous. I think you should stay. I have a good hotel. Very cheap.'

'No, we must go,' I said.

'You have to go tomorrow?' he asked.

'Today,' I replied.

'But you have only just arrived. Why are you going? There is nowhere else to stay.'

107

'There are villages.'

'Yes, but no hotels. The people are very simple.'

'No problem,' I said, imitating a phrase I had heard a million times on the trip so far. 'But which way is good?' Chhom looked at me.

'Padum to Leh is good?' I asked.

'Dangerous. Much snow, very bad.'

'Padum to Kargil is good?' I tried.

'Dangerous, much snow, bad.'

It all seemed to hinge on 'very bad' or 'bad'. Not that Ados and I would have changed our minds on the verdict of one man. Kargil was where we had agreed to go.

We soon left Padum behind and, after fifteen miles of sharp wind in our faces, we reached the village of Phe, where we decided to overnight. Here a family wanted to charge fifty rupees for food and bed. That was about three times the usual rate we'd been paying – the most blatant rip-off since Kathmandu.

The house was notable for its inside loo – a very good idea considering how cold it can get at about 11,500 feet. I'm tempted to describe it as 'nothing to write home about': it was, after all, only a slit in the floor of a tiny empty room – but here I am writing about it. All the junk falls (hopefully) through the slit to the ground where, presumably, it lies until carted away as fertiliser. In warmer mountain areas there are pigs and dogs to eat the swill, but there are no pigs here and very few dogs.

As if to prove to us that this was inhospitable country, it snowed while we slept, coming right into the house through the large square smoke hole in the central living room.

Apart from a bit of a sore head (probably from drinking some of the local spirit), I was feeling quite fit and content. The mother of this house, on the other hand, was coughing like mad to clear her lungs and I couldn't help thinking how lucky I was to be me. Was it birthright or luck or hard work or fate or geographical fact that made people different?

It was a very tough question for 5.30 in the morning, so I rolled over and started prodding my several-layered blister and feeling my tender big toe in preparation for moving off. It had been a real swine since Almora and had seriously affected my performance. Ados, on the other hand, was striding briskly across the mountains. He'd been the strongest for weeks while I just didn't seem able to get on top again.

24

The Mountain Twins

Adrian: I let Dick do the honours on the snowy approach to the Pensi La. Up the Stod River valley, the pass at 15,000 feet was the last major climbing obstacle in our way. I followed my brother through the snow field, stepping in the deep holes his feet left. It was tiring and tense work. The sun had weakened the snow crust and, with each step, we were liable to plunge through. We did so, quite frequently, up to our knees.

We appeared to have run out of habitation and dark thoughts were looming: 'After thirty-six hours we turn back,' I shouted rather dramatically to Dick. Thirty six was the number of hours we allowed for safety in the event of the need for retreat.

'This is daft,' he replied. 'I don't know what the hell happened to Abran and Accha.' They were two villages we'd expected to reach just before our climb out of the Zanskar valley and about thirty miles from Padum.

It was 5.30 in the afternoon. The sun would have set within an hour. We were cold and, worst of all, wet. Feet felt freezing.

'Bloody hell, I thought this was meant to be a piss-easy pass! It's not meant to be deep in snow now,' I complained, taking over the lead from Dick.

Up to now we'd been fortunate whenever we pressed on to prove our principle that if you keep going something will turn up. But it looked as though we were plodding for another bivouac and neither of us wanted one. More frightening (because we could handle one night out) was the prospect of two nights in the open with our meagre stuff. What if the weather broke? What if we had a snowstorm? What if we had to retreat in three feet of snow? How long could our cold wet feet keep frostbite at bay? How long did it take to freeze!

I had been anxious before, but I hadn't been as tight with anxiety as I was then. Running the Himalayas was not worth – well, it wasn't a matter of life and death. I had much more to live for – Karen to marry, a future to find, other mountains to climb. We weren't on a suicide mission but maybe, perhaps, it was just possible that today our calculated risk would collapse on us.

'We'd better look for somewhere to stop pretty soon. How about now?' Dick called. We stood freezing in the snow and considered the options. Ahead of us was a steep side valley running down from the mountains. That gully might have a bit of shelter. We found the dirty snow that signified the buried track and followed it to a shallow stream bed where, delight upon delight, the track spanned it with a bridge. Not only that, but the bridge was made of wood. We stripped the bridge and with

Boy Scout ingenuity built a tiny flat shelter, cementing the gaps with rocks and icy snow.

Sitting in soft falling snow we ate our supper – a thumbnail of tsampa, half a chapati, and the ever-present malaria pills. Soon I squirmed into our foxhole. Feeling like a contortionist, I wrestled with my sleeping bag in the confined shelter seven feet long, two feet high and three feet wide. When my wet shoes and socks were off and I was securely cuddled into my duvet and sleeping bag, I called Dick inside. In the still air of our sealed shelter we hoped to be able to warm ourselves.

By the time we had struggled into sleeping position we were warmed enough to share out one of our two remaining tsampa balls and fall asleep.

Richard: 'How does Ados manage it,' I thought. 'It's freezing and uncomfortable and he is still asleep. I hope he's not frozen to death.' He wasn't – just lying fast asleep as I turned and twisted. My aching limbs seemed to be hammered by the frozen ground beneath and my only comfort, the small oblong of Karrimat 10 inches by 12 inches, had slid to one side where I left it. Recovering it would involve slipping an arm out of the bag and letting all the cold air in.

Ados had said at dusk that it would be only twelve hours until dawn. Only! It seemed a lifetime as I dozed fitfully through it. Always on the verge of being wide awake. I was woken for the final time by a pale luminescence that signalled daytime through the icy cement of our shelter.

I could stand the cold no longer and had to get us moving as fast as possible. I crawled out and stood up in the crystal cold morning air. To my relief only an inch of snow had fallen and I could appreciate how peaceful the land was. How beautiful it was to be alive in it.

Ados shoved the gear out of the tiny entrance and then huffed and puffed to drag himself out too. Once out of our den the wet gear from yesterday began to freeze. My cotton trousers that I had not worn in bed crackled as I pulled them on. Shoelaces stuck out like skinny fingers from their eyelets. My toes and fingers were sharply painful with the cold but at least they were not numb.

Adrian: Dick lagged on the final climb to the pass. Straight up the snow slope we headed. He had had a bad night and was now moving poorly. Every few steps he would swear about the lack of traction in his shoes on the hard snow. He was absolutely right, they had lost their grip, but this was what Running the Himalayas was all about. Making do with what we had, linking widely different climbs and climes into one long journey, tackling each section with the same minimum weaponry.

Concentrating, I stamped my way up the last confusing undulations until I reached a point where the view suddenly opened up: the top! Dick followed, swearing and sweating with the exertion. He was as tired as I had ever seen him all journey and this was probably due to lack of sleep rather than sheer physical effort. We staggered over to sit on the dry rocks of the rough square cairn that marked the summit.

I gazed around and took in the panorama. It was magnificent. Jagged white and

110

silent peaks stretched into the distance under a ceiling of pale brown clouds. Probably that colour because of my tinted glasses! On one side we could look directly up a wide valley laid with a perfect glacier. Its striations of dark rock on white ice gave it the stretched look of multicoloured toffee drawn out from one's teeth. The end of the glacier looked like a glowing blue snout out of which issued a stream. Looking the other way, up the valley, a 22,000-foot peak stood sentinel.

'If this were the only thing to remember, then the whole trip would still be worthwhile,' I said. Dick didn't answer. I fished in my pocket and found what I had been looking for. 'Here you are, a little treat for making it out of Padum.' I gave him a boiled sweet I had carried all the way from Padum for just this moment. 'It's downhill from here to Kargil, and you know what Kargil means!'

I flicked a gesture down the pass in the direction of Padum. 'Long live Kargil!' I yelled, and set off waving my fist triumphantly.

Things went even better with the Pensi La behind us. The vigorous climb had warmed us but we were abominably hungry and eager to get to the next bit of habitation at Ringdom Gompa. We weren't sure how many more hours away that was.

Then suddenly we bumped into what was, for me, one of the most uplifting experiences of the journey.

'What lucky buggers we are!' I exclaimed in my diary, written then and there. It described how we had come down from the summit and found a family heading for Zanskar who had spent the night in a crude dry-stone shelter.

They were four, a man called Lobsan Ringen and his wife, their baby son Nurgu Tulma and their nephew. Plus a couple of horses. Without having to ask (although perhaps looking as though we were about to) we were offered a meal.

'We complain about wet shoes, wet socks, wet gloves, freezing hands, freezing feet, empty stomachs. But here we are having a picnic with Zanskaris at 14,000 feet! We are totally surrounded by snowy mountains, eating salt tea and tsampa. Wonderful!'

We enjoyed one of our best picnics ever. When you're cold, hungry and tired, unexpected food and friendship is priceless. We offered Lobsan Ringen money which he refused, so to emphasise our gratitude we gave him the only presents we could spare – two safety pins.

In return he gave us a handful of barley grains for our pockets. I was touched and went on invigorated. Adrian was already on something of a high and, as he coasted on with me behind him, a feeling of peace came over him.

He had risen above the cold and misty level of hardship, pain and discomfort, and with absolute confidence knew that he could cope with them. Hunger and fatigue held no fears. He had reached, in mountain metaphor, 'a summit of achievement' and he was 'in the sun watching the great peaks of experience slide by'. Ahead of him he could see 'a ridge of pride and, standing high, the pinnacle of unexpected success'. Beyond that were 'the foothills of happiness – far away, too far to see their extent but I was certain that I could see the way to go.' He saw too, the mountains as

111

symbols of higher ideals and resolved to strive that high. Meanwhile we had to get on, our eyes on the prize.

The thing about travelling, even when you can see what's ahead, is that it can be further away than you think. We entered the wide Suru Valley and, there in the middle of a plain, was the outline of the 200-year-old Ringdom Gompa on a small hill. Our next bowl of tsampa looked less than half-an-hour away.

Adrian: But we had been misled by the size of the country: the little mound with its small building was a great mount on which stood the huge rambling structure of the monastery. A Himalayan Mont St Michel, square and solid in a sea of alluvium and snow. Two hours after we had first seen it, we arrived at the foot of the hill and took the winding path up to the door. A sign said 'Brekfust, lunch and dinar with Lamas' but there was no sign of life. We banged on the door and yelled and whistled. No reply. Dick set off around the walls in one direction while I went the other. My side soon petered out over a little crag, so I returned to find Dick.

'If this means that the whole valley may be deserted we'll be in trouble,' said Dick. I shouted some more. A little head appeared over the wall, wearing a maroon cap with pointed sides. An old monk, he indicated we should return along the wall to the door that we had come from. We waited. With a clang the bolt was thrown and the big door creaked open. The bent old guy beckoned us in. Once inside, he shuffled us into a courtyard and showed us where he had been sitting when he heard our yells, and where he had been able to stand and look down on us, outside. He was the only one there.

He smiled and in gentle gestures set about describing the building, pointing out the flags on the roof and doors and windows that led into this room and that room. Eventually he took us down a dark corridor off the courtyard and we were ushered into a small room with a sleeping area and below the small window, a sitting and cooking place: his cell.

The monk settled cross-legged by the fire and slid a pan above the embers. Dick and I lay back against the wall and breathed a sigh of relief. Warmth and drink and food were almost with us.

Placing one finger on his chest the monk said: 'Head lama'. He then proceeded to explain that most of the monastery's residents were away for the winter. Only he and four others had stayed the whole year and his four companions were visiting the closest village for supplies and news. They should be back today.

He had only tea and tsampa to offer, but he was very happy to share it with us. His tea-making was gracious and practised as befitted an important man for whom this was one of life's few practicalities. Tsampa, though, was less of a ritual and the bowl he placed between us was there to be dug into as and when and how we wished. I made sloppy tsampa soup with my tea while Dick copied the monk and made solid tsampa balls, which he ate with sips of the hot oily tea. The only difference in Dick's style was that he increased the quantities tenfold!

The monk wanted to know about our travels and our destination, why we were travelling in the winter. We tried to explain.

'More tea?' He smiled and lapsed into silence after the effort of our conversation.

Outside it was cold, windy, grey and bleak. Comfortless. Inside the lama's cell we had everything: tea, tsampa, warmth, a rug to sit on, a light for when it got dark. It was all a man needed and, during our journey, we had come to appreciate these simple things. But it was still unreal, like being in a play. We knew that, barring disaster, we would be stumbling back to civilisation. Suddenly it would not be enough to have just warmth and light and food and water; I would want light with a lampshade, central heating, steak medium to well-done, water mixed not with iodine but with the right brand of whisky and tea in my favourite cup.

When we started out on our expedition, it was supposed to be 'the expedition to end all expeditions'. It was meant to fulfil our needs for adventure and physical effort and leave us free from dreams to pursue normal lives: take a good job, make a career, be family men, keep up with Mr Jones. But when we sat in a place like this monastery, my thoughts did not fit that plan. I was tending to question the Western values that Dick had been debunking for some time: I was beginning to find pleasure in the bare necessities of life, and satisfaction in hardship. And I wondered if I would reap half the pleasure from luxuries again.

Before the trip we had joked that we might find some religious truths and return as different men. Now I can understand why others have travelled to far off places and returned changed. I had never believed it would happen to me (indeed I had prayed it would not!) but at that moment, in a monastery stuck in what some might describe as a Godforsaken plain, and in front of the head lama, I no longer felt the same.

Richard: Ados was, according to the most obvious diagnosis, having an attack of idealism, brought on by symptoms of euphoria. It verged on a significant spiritual experience. Indeed, later that day, he suggested that perhaps there really was 'some kind guy above who is keeping us out of trouble'. That night even I was less sceptical about that 'kind guy'.

We stood outside our host's stable, pissing into the tussocky grass. Above, the stars were bright and clean, the mountains just blacker pieces of sky. A feeling of *déjà-vu* came over me, as though I'd been here before.

'You know what you were saying,' I said, 'about someone looking after us? Well, I'd say that was closer to possible now than I've ever thought before.'

In this mood, free from anxiety, we certainly saw the world a little differently. An increasing generosity of spirit started to shine in the diaries and Adrian, at least in his head if not in his cursory writings, drew symbolic meanings from the things around him.

Adrian: As we approached Zolidok with a young villager, we passed a small group that were making their way toward the monastery. We were about one hundred yards away from them on this wide and silent plain. They shouted to our man who yelled out in reply. The exchange went on as we drew further apart – the shouts growing fainter and fainter, leaving echoes in the mind.

To me, we were like spacecraft, passing in the vastness of space, acknowledging each other and reaffirming our togetherness without having to deviate from our path. Without understanding a word, I had a notion I knew what it was all about. And it was good.

113

The valley leading away from Zolidok became narrow and deep with steep walls of loose rock on either side. The river, which during the thaw thundered down the centre, was quiet and hidden beneath thick snow. Rockfalls and debris from the slopes were spread across the valley floor so that making a route was exhausting and frustrating.

We would stumble through deep snow and then drag ourselves onto a huge rock, cross it and leap back into the cold snow again. Sometimes plunging down waist deep, we would have to squirm out of our holes.

It seemed as if the nasty powers-that-be were determined to try one last trick. As we struggled down the valley, the sun rose and the snow became softer. The sides of the valley steepened and towered over us. The floor narrowed to a mighty V. We were forced to climb along the side of the valley, crossing steep snow slopes that swept down to the river. Dick's shoes had little purchase on the snow and he had to be sure that every step would hold on the icy surface.

I had time to admire the great sweeps of white and the glacier snouts that poked over the shoulder on the far side of the valley. Above us at 25,000 feet were the summits of the mountain twins, Nun and Kun: but we couldn't see them for dark clouds. It was all rather menacing. Rocks crashed down the slopes, leaping and bouncing and spouting plumes of dust and snow but one thought reinforced my skills: 'Yea, though I walk through the valley of the shadow of death, I shall fear no evil.'

25

Zolidok to Srinigar

Adrian: We had come nine hours from Zolidok and on Day 85 stood on a narrow ridge separating two worlds. Behind us, Nun and Kun, the one peak snow-white, the other black-rock, raised their twin heads above the rest, overlooking the hostile land through which we'd been travelling for ten days.

After a hundred rocky miles of ice-grey rivers, sharp blue skies and patchy snowfields by dull-desert scrub, we could see below us the softer valley of the Suru river, and its lush-green fields flowered in yellow, white and purple. But not only was the landscape different. We'd left the lonely bastions of the Buddhist faith, the prayers blowing in the wind. We were entering the Islamic atmosphere of north-west Ladakh and the touchy territory between India and Pakistan. It was a whole new scene.

We sped down the slope, skating over patches of slippery snow towards the track to Parkatchik. Dick slipped and landed heavily on his backside and I laughed uproariously until his swearing stopped me. We went on more soberly until we reached the village, a little apprehensive about the reception we'd receive from the Muslim people.

From my time in Arabia I was aware of the rather inflexible attitude of the Believers and the custom which inclined to keep the womenfolk out of contact with strange men. I was afraid that, because of this, we would not be entertained as freely as we had been up till then. But after a group of villagers had understood our request for food, we were led by an old man to his house.

Inside, a woman squatting by a fire seemed quite pleased to see us and we were soon enjoying a snack of tea and tsampa. We gathered that they thought we were going on to Kargil, only ten miles away, but we persuaded them with an offer of payment to put us up for the night.

A two-rupee note had also induced our hosts to produce some sugar for our tea. It was not much more than a stir in a tea cup but it started Dick's hang-up about being back in a 'money society' and all the mercenary evils he connected with the progress of the motor road, which we'd now reached. In the wilds of Zanskar, the people shared their simple food with us not expecting the payment we offered them when we moved on, but now my brother anticipated the irritations of a section in which money talked. On the eighty-fifth day of our traverse he was exclaiming: 'I hate civilisation! I hate money!'

115

That night we stayed in a poor house. A very old man appeared to live on a bed in the kitchen and his only activity, it seemed, was to turn to the wall, spit as high as he could and then watch the spittle dribble down. In the candlelight we could see the wall was wildly flecked. Speaking of food, our host told us that the month-long Muslim festival of Ramadam would be starting in a few days time when the new moon rose. During this period, Muslims are forbidden food during the day, and it occurred to us that we would run into a problem. The man even suggested that we should also observe the fast.

The following morning we headed for Kargil, and after an abortive attempt to ford the ice-cold river barefoot and trying what the locals described as a 'dirty dirty' track, we did the wise thing and followed the main way to Kargil. There a rickety sign board proclaimed it the District Capital.

Once an important junction in the trade routes, Kargil had lost its rank because the politics of the region have closed the way to Pakistan and Tibet. Nevertheless it was one of the most significant towns on our list. Even if we did not take another step we could claim we'd completed a traverse of the Himalayas. It called for some sort of celebration.

We found the Yak Tail, a restaurant with a menu, and settling down to 86 rupees worth (£5.50) of meal, we allowed ourselves a congratulatory pat on the back. With some pride we discovered we were the first travellers to come out of Zanskar that season, and the locals were amazed that we had made it from Padum.

The owner of the place wrote in our log book that this had been the worst winter in living memory and that he was extremely surprised to see two young men, equipped so lightly, come from the south. But it was true. We had arrived and all the travail had been worth while. We were the first people to get through this year. Now we only had to get to Srinigar, Gulmarg and Rawalpindi – and it would all be over.

We took the road to Srinigar, 204 kilometres away, feeling strong. We were bolstered by our achievement, freed of the burden of failure and the fear of losing. After so long in pursuit of what had seemed an unreachable goal, I revelled in a sense of security.

We soon notched up the northern-most point of our traverse and hurried on, aiming to reach Srinigar in four days, before the close of business on Friday. It was now Day 87 and, with a bit of luck and a plane ride across the border, we could make Rawalpindi on the hundredth day. Unable to penetrate the Cease-Fire boundary between the two countries, that was the best we could do. It would break our foot-powered traverse, but we were reconciled to that because we had established Gulmarg as our prime finishing point. After that, the rules changed and, as far as we were concerned, Rawalpindi would be a bonus.

Richard: Downhill but not a doddle. That is what we thought as we tackled the road to the end. Like Ados, I was also motivated by our success and even acknowledged the advantages of roads. For one thing, the road was easy to follow and we were unencumbered by the problems of cross-country trekking – the path and foot finding, the dangers of falling rock, the loose stones underfoot, knee-jerking descents and snow clumsy climbs.

116

We didn't have to concentrate on each step and we could plan ahead, plot out a circuit of parties and visits to friends when we got back, and dream up ways to help Intermediate Technology make the most of our venture. We also chatted more, or rather Ados did, flowing on for half an hour at a time, on a fund of stories from his days in Saudi and the States. He's great like this, full of interesting anecdotes. But I never seem to remember mine.

In a burst of self-adulation we also sang our version of *The British Grenadiers*:

> Some talk of Kanchenjunga and some of Taplejung
> Of Leh and Lamayuru and travels such as these
> But of all the world's great traverse teams,
> There's none that can compare
> With a ta ra ra, ra woh row woh
> To this British Running Pair.

We ground to earth with a bump that night. Once again we ran out of daylight. Thinking we'd easily find warmth, food and shelter, we found only shelter – a shed of sorts which we shared with the remains of a bicycle. For all our supercharged ideas about ourselves, it still wasn't all free-wheeling.

Adrian: One and a half days south-west of Kargil we were within reach of the Zoji La, at 11,500 feet the last major pass before Srinigar. Not a steep pass from the northern approach, it is the escape route from Ladakh, the gateway to the Vale of Kashmir. For some freakish reason it is also extremely reluctant to shed its winter snow and the road over it was still not open for vehicles. We made our way up the pass, gaining altitude imperceptibly.

As the evening of Day 88 came, we began to look for shelter. At 10,000 feet we didn't relish the thought of another night out. We were ten miles beyond Drass near a point marked on the map as Pendrass when Dick pointed to a dark shape that turned out to be a hut close to the track. Dick stuck his head around the door and slipped inside. I followed. We found ourselves among four men who looked bewildered as I tried to explain our arrival in pidgin Hindi and hand signs.

'I am Captain Rama with the Indian army,' said a man sitting cross-legged on one of the beds. 'We are honoured to meet you. My home town is Calcutta. Have you been there?'

'No, we haven't,' I replied and, turning to Dick, I sighed: 'Wonderful, now we've got involved with the Army.'

We had been struck by the strong military presence in the area since reaching Kargil. Every few miles we came across soldiers, vehicles, military compounds and plaques commemorating the soldiers who'd fallen in India's battles with its neighbour. We had also discussed the chances of being picked up and had decided to avoid any risk by steering clear of anything military. Now here we were bumming a bed off them.

The captain was courteous and assured us that we could stay. To put the anxiety

117

we must have been showing to rest, he said that he wouldn't even mention us when he made his next report to headquarters. But he did.

' 'Allo, 'allo . . . this is Captain Rama reporting,' he was speaking into a phone. 'I have two Inglishmen here . . .'

In a mixture of English and long bursts of Hindi, he continued his report and we gathered he was getting instructions about us. But what was going on? Did HQ want to see us, would we be taken to Srinigar? My imagination reared alarming notions and Dick and I exchanged worried glances. The thought of a few hours interrogation with the Indian Army would, in other circumstances, have been positively amusing, but now we couldn't afford the time, and worse still we did not, absolutely did not, want to end up riding in a vehicle.

'You must stay with us for the night,' said Captain Rama. It sounded like an offer we couldn't refuse and, hardly reassured that the man was simply being hospitable, we muttered our thanks.

In due course Dick commandeered the only light in the hut, a hurricane lamp, to write his diary. He was unperturbed by the fact that one of the chaps was studying a sheet of paper. I fell asleep trying to calculate the chances of a midnight escape, imagining I was one of those cloaked figures glancing worriedly over their shoulders, who have to flee their captors across the desert wastes of so many fairy tales.

Over the Zoji La, we entered the Vale of Kashmir, historically and scenically one of the most romantic areas of all India. Ever since the days of the Moghul Emperors in the sixteenth century it has been known as the 'Pearl of the Himalayas' and our first view of it coincided with all the tourist brochures that blurb about the beauty of the land.

A couple of miles below the summit we met forty army trucks. The convoy had stopped and the crews had gathered at a memorial stone perched on some very steep screes. They burnt incense sticks and put up flags in a sensitive remembrance ceremony for, we gathered, a similar convoy that six or seven years ago lost some men and thirty-two trucks when a section of the road gave way.

In Sonamarg, one of the colonial Hill Stations, we found the tourists, many of whom were waiting for transport to take them into Ladakh now that the snows had just melted. These people were anathema to Dick and he waxed sarcastic about them in his diary:

'Oh, how absolutely wonderful to be an intrepid tourist in quaint dirty little India!' he wrote. 'This place is completely swamped by lovely white-faced westerners ethnically sipping sugar tea and exploring those fascinating curio shops full of rural handicrafts. The clothes these rich foreigners sport is a joke: ethnic hats and bright blue beads, jazzy jackets and Kashmir shawls casually slung over shoulders, denim jeans, Indian thongs. There are men with earrings, women with crew-cuts and everyone here has an "I-am-trendier-than-thou" expression.'

Heaven knows what we or our expressions looked like, for we felt distinctly superior to this lot. After all, hadn't we just come across the Zoji La from Darjeeling! As for Dick's sentiments about the tourists, I shared some of these, but I couldn't get so worked up about them. Not when everything seemed so under control.

For me it was all plain sailing but suddenly, in sight of the finish, Dick was going through a whole gamut of moods and emotion. From feelings of depression and affection for me – ('The only nice thing that happened to me today was travelling with Ados') – through outbursts of utter frustration or exhilaration, to moments of humour, sentiment and manic description in his diary, Dick was on an emotional see-saw. I mean, have you ever seen a twenty-nine-year-old Cumbrian cry? It was almost as though, having kept a grip on himself for so long, he could, at last, let go.

Some way out of Sonamarg we went for a cross-country line to cut out ten miles of the road which loops round to Srinigar. This took us up the Hayan La, at 10,000 feet positively the last piddling pass before Srinigar, now only about twenty miles away. To make it interesting, it was raining and Dick's shoes were worn absolutely smooth on the bottom. To make it worse, there was no path and the whole mountainside was loose earth, pine needles, dead wood and slippery slate. The end of the day was closing in.

Struggling to make the ridge, Dick was slipping and sliding all over the place, and the volume of his swearing increased as the climb grew stiffer. I, with my healthier treads, was having an easier time and I coaxed him along but couldn't do anything about his technique, which took him four steps up and three slides back. It was Snakes and Ladders without any ladders. Then he fell, got up, slid back onto his hands and knees, crawled a little further, screamed in anger, accused me of goading him, fell again and sat there crying with frustration and maligning the whole world for turning on him.

Of course, he made it in the end, and on the ridge we took stock, thanked God and Andy Fox – a man we'd met in Sonamarg who'd given us a Mars bar.

Dick's arms, knees and bum were covered in mud and muck. He'd also cut his hand on a rock. He was exhausted and all he wanted was some safety with a little warmth and food thrown in. What happened next, Dick describes in his diary:

'Okay, tell me this, how the heck does the Lord do it? He's put me here on a ridge at dusk at 10,000 feet in tears because I'm knackered, my shoes are no good, it's cold and raining, we can't see where the hell to go and all the damn houses and safety are down in the valleys 4000 feet below us. So what does He do? I'll tell you. He blows harder so it gets colder, then He lets out an almighty crack that splits our eardrums and sends a yellow streak across the sky which blows a hole in the heavenly water pipes. The rain comes pelting down. We have no option but to move on, drawn towards a noise in the mist as though mesmerised by the angelic host. What are we imagining we hear? Birds? Sheep? The wind? But no, it's a tranny radio wrapped up in a tent with people around it. Up here in the pouring rain, the Lord has kindly arranged for us an encampment of Kashmiris heading for the hills further north. The most beautiful Kashmiri mother, with the sweetest Kashmiri children, beckons us into the best-ever tent for the most excellent tea and chapatis we have ever eaten. Lord, we are thankful for this and all other mercies. But especially for this.'

The tent actually wasn't the 'best ever'; it was full of smoke and chock-a-block with family. So we went on down, slithering and cursing once more until, at 8.30, we reached some houses and were taken in.

On reflection, I was a little shaken by Dick's performance on the mountain. It was the first time that either of us had let the physical problems really get to us. It made

119

me wonder how close we had been to pushing ourselves into serious situations in the more dangerous places we'd struggled through. What if we'd been hit, not just by rain and a slippery slope within spitting distance of Srinigar, but by a blizzard, say on the Shingo La? Would we have panicked? Could we have pulled ourselves together and got through?

There were no answers to these questions. The dangers were now behind us. After so many 'last' obstacles since the Shingo La, we had finally arrived at the very last. So Dick could afford to indulge in a little tantrum.

Richard; My last 'ethnic' night wasn't exactly one to savour, but it was memorable. Our house was a largish, partially divided room with clay walls and a flat, thatched roof. It had two old men, a fine-featured woman, two young boys and a baby, a calf tied to a bed, a cow at the door and a basket of chickens on the floor. It also had an electric light – a bare bulb that burned all night and had me tossing and turning. It didn't seem to bother the family, their calf or Ados but the cow shifted from one foot to the other and I had some sympathy for her. At 4 am I got fed up and went outside. Ten miles away I could see all the lights of Srinigar.

Back inside I lay in my bag and took advantage of the artificial light to write my diary. Around me the family began to stir and mess about. 'The sound like a water tap which you heard just then,' I wrote, 'is the cow pissing on the floor.' I mean, really! But I added it wasn't insanitary because 'it's all soaked up by the dry cow-dung and straw on the floor; which then sticks to your feet and is carried outside!'

Soon the chickens were chirping away, a few fowls clucking, one of the boys was stroking the calf and the woman was milking the cow. She gave us each a bowl of dark maroon salt tea called Namkin Char and a handful of hot powdered flour to go with it. My helping floated for a couple of seconds, spread across the surface, then sank to a sludge on the bottom of the bowl. We drank the tea, then tipped the sludge and leaves into our mouth. Taking our cue from our hosts, we chewed most of the leaves and spat the hard bits on the floor in front of us. All in all a very good starter to the day.

It was our turn next to amuse our friends and it occurred to me how odd our habits must have seemed to these and all the other people with whom we had stayed. We struggled (out of modesty) to put on our trousers inside our big blue plastic bags. We wiped white grease – our antiseptic cream – on our sunburnt lips and noses. Then we worked on our feet. I examined mine minutely, assessing the state of each blister, each toe, and the spread of my athlete's foot. We beat and massaged our stiff hydroscopic socks to soften them so that they would go on more easily; we compressed our voluminous sleeping bags and duvet jackets into footballs and shoved them away and then, what must be the most alarming act of all, I sat down, stuck my fingers in my eyes and cried. Then smiled. With my contacts in, I was ready for another go at the world.

Before we could leave, the father nipped out and returned a few minutes later with a big smile and pocketsful of red and yellow cherries for us. We ate them on the way and they tasted good but it's the generosity I savoured most.

Our entry into Srinigar was barely noticed. No one seemed to waste more than a glance on us and I decided the Kashmiris must have seen their fair share of peculiar Europeans over the last fifteen years or so. Nevertheless, it was a bit of a let down to find we just melted into the throng. We had half-hoped there would have been a greeting of sorts.

We padded on sore feet into the centre of the town before we succumbed to the temptations of a snack bar, some sticky pastry for me and some longed-for coffee for Ados.

The city we had just entered was by far the biggest since Kathmandu, square miles larger than either Tanakpur or Almora. There was a large suburban-type sprawl before we started hitting the main noise, which is louder than can be imagined. You really need a tape to record the decibels in the chaotic medley of bells and bustle, the hooting, hammering and jabbering. You also need a smell machine to capture the atmosphere impregnated with curry flavours, seasoned with wafts of sewage, diesel fumes and more than a pinch of dust. But you don't need a sensitive eye to see how fascinating the town can be for visitors, how picturesque the Moghul gardens, the labyrinth of waterways, the famous houseboats on Dal Lake or the Jhelum River which winds its sluggish path through the town.

There are four million people in Kashmir and half a million of them are in Srinigar, the principal city. For centuries it has received flocks of visitors from the south, most of them Hindus, making their pilgrimage to the holy ice-cave of Amarnath in the direction of the Zoji La.

There is a saying that 'Kashmiris are so fond of the truth they will never part with it', and the same could be said for their land. When Europeans started coming to Kashmir, a law, still in force, was introduced forbidding foreigners to own property and at one time they weren't even allowed to build. However, the colonial Brits who preferred their Indian summers to be cool, had a way round that problem. They built their holiday homes on the water! Since 1888 when the first one was floated, they have become monuments to Victorian ingenuity, a feature of Srinigar. To stay in one (they come in varying degrees of luxury) is one of the attractions for the tourist. Apart from their novelty value they also take you out of the hassle and bustle of the city centre.

We made our way to one of these, the *Star of Zanzibar*, on which the Mountain Travel firm have their office. Srinigar was one of our equipment dumps and Lisa and Nick Van Gruisen had arranged for Mountain Travel to keep our gear there. The two bags were waiting for us and a bedroom as well.

Here we washed and bathed, sorted through our new gear and finally put our feet up on soft beds.

'I reckon we've made it,' I said.

That afternoon we had to organise our flight to Pakistan, and then the next day, crawl on to Gulmarg. Unbelievably, it was Day 91 and we only had twenty-seven miles to go!

26

End of an Adventure

We're on our way to Gulmarg, we shall not be moved,
We're on our way to Gulmarg, we shall not be moved,
We are the team that's going to win the Traverse Cup,
We shall not be moved.

Another of our songs of praise. True to its spirit, we were up early on the 92nd Day and on our way to Gulmarg. Just like any old Indian Hill Station to most people but a very special place to us. It lies west of Nanga Parbat and marks the end of our continuous foot traverse east to west past all the fourteen 8000 metre peaks in the world. It was going to be a momentous day.

We made our first stop twenty-three kilometres outside Srinigar at Magam. By three o'clock, when we reached Tangmarg, we had technically passed Nanga Parbat, our last 8000-metre peak but like the batsman who hits a six when he has scored his century just in case the scorer's got it wrong, we were going on to Gulmarg. Besides people have heard of Gulmarg because at 9000 feet above sea level it has the highest golf course in the world! It made for a better finish.

At 3.30 we started up the last hill to the end of our journey in India. Our sprint up it was our final fling before we broke an imaginary tape.

At 4.15 I made a brief diary entry: 'DONE IT!' Scrawled all over the page.

We celebrated with a drink of water and some glucose biscuits – only one – and I promised myself no more glucose biscuits for me, never ever ever!

'It's bloody easy, this traverse lark, let's go back the same way,' I said.

'Yeah, let's do that,' said my brother.

Just a hundred yards from our main-street finish, we looked north-east and saw a sea of cloud surmounted by a white massif that was Nanga Parbat. It was one of the most satisfying sights in the world, and we had come 2000 miles and climbed 280,000 feet over 65 mountain passes in ninety-two days to enjoy it.

'How do you feel?' asked Ados and I didn't really know. There was the satisfaction but I didn't feel wildly elated.

'It's difficult to say,' I said. 'I'll need time to analyse my thoughts on getting here. I feel as though I've reached the end but there's still a long way to go.'

'Yeah, I know what you mean, and I feel a bit sad it's all over,' said Ados. 'It feels a bit like arriving at the summit of a mountain and then not being able to enjoy the experience because you have to face the problem of survival again, just getting down. We can't even start to work out what it all means to us.'

However before we could start to do anything else, we still had to finish the journey from Darjeeling to Rawalpindi. We had told everyone back in England that we would do it, so being men to our words we had to do it.

To get back to Srinigar, we hired a couple of horses to ride down the hill. It was an exciting and bumpy sensation. It was also weird not to be on foot while travelling.

In Tangmarg we hired a clapped out rattle trap of a jeep and raced along at a scary twenty miles an hour! We passed the baker who had sold us some sesame seed biscuits, the boy with the stale rolls, the old man still immobile sitting on his steps and the same road gang now putting down their shovels. I might have been in a time machine going backwards over my life. But that went only as far as Srinigar.

There we met Gary Whitby whom IT had sent over to and fuel the publicity machine for our Rawalpindi finish. We told him we would end it all on June 27th, Day 101. And then we ate.

The following day, Day 93, we flew from Srinigar to Amritsar. At the airport we weighed ourselves. Ados stood at 140 pounds, I at 146 pounds.

'Christ!' I exclaimed. 'That's only ten stone six pounds – I've never weighed that in my life!'

This was one-and-a-half stone less than my weight in Darjeeling. Even though the illness would account for some of the loss, my amazement was still understandable because even at the age of ten I weighed in at ten stone. I was a fatty in those days and full of puppy innocence. Since then I had changed radically. The boy who once believed his father had climbed Mount Everest had been to its foot himself. I now questioned everything in sight, including, sometimes, myself.

I had also changed from the lad who had hidden behind conformity to become a man who demonstrated his individuality and was quite happy to be an oddity.

As a boy, I had always regarded myself as the norm. When I was at the bottom of the class, I assumed that all normal people must be thick. Then after I had climbed to the top of the class, I decided that anyone could do it if they worked. As for running the Himalayas, well 'anyone' could also do that if they put their minds to it.

I proved to myself that I could keep going, even when I was so ill and perhaps should have stopped to get strong again. As it was, my head-down determination cost me my psychological and physical advantage over my younger brother. Ados, in his own remarkable way, surged to the lead.

'Ados is totally outlasting me on this one hundred day journey', I wrote when we had reached Pakistan. And I was reviewing our performance: 'I came from England much fitter and stronger with a record of personal bests a whole length better than Ados. I stayed in front up to Kathmandu and, in my keenness, set too fast a pace from Everest Base Camp and burnt him out. However, after he had recovered in Arughat Bazar and we set off across the back of Annapurna with me taking pills for dysentery, he started to pull ahead. I'll always remember plodding blankly in his footsteps up the Thorong La.

'We equalised in West Nepal when the enormity of our trek hit us, but Ados recovered and strode ahead through the Indian Kumaon foothills. I haven't caught up again; I am always trailing behind watching his brisk steps and dreaming head while I hobble painfully behind.

'I am nearly recovered today but I doubt I can break him with only a few days to the end of our physical adventure. I wonder how the aftermath will pan out? The press conferences, articles, the book? People along the route already assume that I am the younger brother. Will I be able to hold my share of the fun?'

Now I had started to worry that Ados might dominate the 'aftermath'. Even here, my competitive streak was showing and I was determined to re-assert myself when we got back to England. It wasn't that important for Adrian. He had found his worth but not necessarily in competition with me.

'The whole thing ended very even,' says Adrian. 'Neither of us had more to do with the success than the other.'

That might be so – one couldn't have done it without the other – but even being level with me was a step up for Ados at first. Then, when he took over, he enjoyed the experience of leading from the front, and the responsibilities reinforced his confidence to a point where he felt the equal of any adventurer.

For all our petty differences during the trial, the bond between us was stronger than we realised, and if the experience did nothing else, it amazed us to find how compatible we were.

Before the expedition, Adrian was closer to our younger brother, Christopher. Which is another way of saying he liked him more, and had Chris been available, he would definitely have come along on an expedition, though not necessarily the Himalayas. In fact, Adrian has never regarded me very much as his friend, as someone who shared similar ideas and reactions and was easy to be with. I came in the category of kin, someone connected accidentally by blood, whom he appreciated and respected. But he wouldn't necessarily choose to go down to the pub with me. Nor I with him.

'Cousin Nick, for instance, is more of a friend,' says Adrian, 'because if I wanted an easy-going pint or two, just sit back and have a dreamy chat about skiing across the Arctic, I'd go with him. Have Dick along and we'd get involved in the philosophy of effort or something. It would be intense and not much fun.'

Thrown together in the mountains, and sharing the thick with the thin, we got to know each other better than we know any other human beings. We grew closer than we thought possible. We leaned on each other: we kept each other warm, kept each other going. We trusted and understood each other. It was also more than that:

'We had moments of pure companionship,' says Ados. 'And the experience of being so at one with another person was terrific. At times we were so pleased with each other we'd collapse on the road in laughter and exclaim "This is great!" Then everything was fun, the sun shone, our aches and pains were muted and we knew there would be a tea house round the corner.'

On Day 93 the tea house round the corner was in Rawalpindi.

From Amritsar, we took a train to Lahore in Pakistan, then a luxury bus to Rawalpindi, booking in at Flashman's Hotel after midnight.

True to form, I attended to my diary:

'We have been thrown straight into the First World today – planes, trains, express coaches, assorted modern cars, neon signs, city clothes, coffee, sandwiches and chips in cafes, time schedules, panic and rush. I have even been subjected to the ultimate ignominy of sitting in the Pakistani equivalent of a UK motoring cafe with two companions who sipped Coca Cola and, with totally blank expressions, watched the highlights of a game of cricket on television and the ads, one of which extolled the virtues of Gold Leaf cigarettes. I don't think I ever want to readjust to television.'

It also took some readjustment getting back into the spirit of the traverse. There was an artificiality to it which we didn't entirely care for. But it was all in a good cause. We needed to get to Rawalpindi as we had initially told IT, and to finish the whole adventure in a glare of publicity. Our main challenge was to make it worthwhile for the press and television which, according to reports, had at last been fired by our achievement.

One idea was that we should take a bus up to the Karakorams to Gilgit, and run back from there. But Gilgit was a considerable distance north of Gulmarg and too far from Rawalpindi for us to be back by Day 101. Our solution was a compromise – we would bus it to Gilgit, back-track by bus again to a point not lower than our east-west line from Gulmarg. This meant that, but for the hop over the border, we would have kept to the line of our traverse and still be in Rawalpindi in time. The problem was that it would bring us to 101 days. We consoled ourselves by saying that this was good news, the expedition was designed to fail anyway!

On Day 95 we set off up the Karakoram Highway for another exhausting, head-achy bus ride. It turned out to be a terrible day. I felt dreadful and spent most of the time lying on the floor of the bus below window-level. We travelled for hours up the Indus Valley before I even saw the river. After fourteen hours, we were so disgruntled that we climbed off at Chilas before reaching Gilgit.

We then caught a bus going south and arrived at Bara-Zherat fourteen hours later after nearly thirty hours on the road. This was on the same latitude as Kargil and 175 kilometres from Rawalpindi. Here, at 4.20 pm on Day 96, we took to our feet once more. But it wasn't the same.

We had done our high-speed traverse of the mountains and we found that this place Rawalpindi was not in the Himalayas but 150 miles away across a hot, dusty plain. But we had to go there.

The major fascination was in coping with Ramadan, the ninth month of the Muslim year, when 'the gates of Paradise are open, the gates of Hell shut and the Devil is in chains.' Mohammed proclaimed that this time should be kept by fasting. According to the law, followers should 'Eat and drink until so much of the dawn appears that a white thread may be distinguished from a black, then keep the fast completely until night.'

We had to rely on biscuits and fruit during the day and litres of water. Round us, the people lazed or meditated away the day. Then activity quickened with approaching sundown and we, like the locals, waited expectantly for the cry from the muezzin to herald a night of eating and drinking.

In the Paris Hotel at Haripur, I couldn't sleep properly for all the din of the night.

My half-awake imagination conjured up a bedlam of nasty little so-and-sos, goblins and gremlins, evil pixies and urchins, 'furry little bundles of pussycats gobbling scraps and mechanical piranha-like fleas'. At 1.30 the noise was too much to bear in the stifling night air so I got up and joined it. I sat with the throng of midnight feasters, tucking into piles of roti and curry.

I postponed eating myself, thinking there was a lot of time to order before dawn. Round 3 am, I was bored with my flagging company and woke Ados. By the time he appeared the tables were nearly empty. Then the siren sounded announcing the start of another day's fast. I calculated it was at least three quarters of an hour earlier than official dawn at 4.30, but there was nothing we could do. We had to pull out all the stops to persuade the proprietor to serve us any food at all.

Later in the day Pakistani television caught up with us and later still the BBC who made arrangements to meet again the next day.

Finding the television and press only interested now that all the real traverse was over left us rather dejected. Our frayed tempers weren't improved by a poor night in a local Youth Hostel. It seemed as though our journey was turning sour. We were hot and irritable. Ados was tempted to take a swipe at me for some petty observation or other, and I told a policeman who asked to see our passports to 'Get Lost'. When the policeman took me by the arm, I shook him off. Fortunately, the Pakistani TV crew arrived in time to prevent an international incident.

We have met any number of kind and friendly people during our traverse. But the worst, the most abusive we have met, are us.

Day 100 was not at all as we'd envisaged it. But it had its memorable moments. We eased our creaking legs into a run for the BBC cameras. Then ITN arrived on the scene and we enjoyed watching the rival crews jockeying for the best stuff. We learned that we'd already made it on BBC's *Grandstand* on Saturday afternoon, as well as all the news broadcasts.

About four miles south of Taxila we clocked up our 100 days travelling since Darjeeling. We knocked up a few celebration poses which gave the Beeb and ITN some bonus material. Then the TV crews dashed back to their air-conditioning and left us to plod on in the dry heat of Pakistan.

Our last night on the road was not without adventure. Mr Munheeradin, secretary to the Minister for Sport, Tourism and Culture, had advised us to stop off at the Tarnaul Police Station on the outskirts of Rawalpindi. There we would be looked after, he had said. We took him at his word.

We imagined mounds of shiny fruit, gallons of hot tea and a table groaning under curries, rice, chapatis and chutneys. We pressed on with bones creaking, throats dry and parched, eyes glazed and bodies oozing sweat. Under the afternoon sun it was like being broiled and baked at the same time. We reached the police post which stands on top of a hillock. It was built of brick and painted brown and yellow. It had a big steel aerial and a compound of big canvas tents to house about forty men. It was very real but the welcome we had been heading for turned into a mirage.

We asked where we would be accommodated, but the answer to that was, 'You go to Islamabad to show your visas.'

We tried explaining who we were, why we were there. We threw names of government ministers at them, showed official letterheads from embassies. The Tarnaul police were adamant we'd come to the wrong address.

'But Mr Munheeradin sent us,' we cried. It didn't mean a thing.

Shaking our angry heads and saying 'what knackers!' we had no option but to cut our losses. We headed back to the village to find an ordinary hotel and ordered a big consolation 100-day meal. We were just getting stuck into that when a very official, important looking Deputy Superintendant of the Pakistani Police burst in. His man at Tarnaul had mistakenly spiked his offer of hospitality and, full of apologies, he wished to put it right. He paid our bill at the hotel and whisked us off in his new Toyota four-wheel drive, back to the Tarnaul Station.

This time there were smiles all round. We are very honoured guests! And fed as such! Our Deputy Super had brought a boot-load of stuff from Islamabad – roast chicken, cakes, fizzy drinks, a huge container of assorted chilled fruits. He even put us into his chief's office for our paperwork and I sat at his desk dripping sweat all over his best chair. 'Sorry,' I said to my diary, 'but I am truly enjoying myself. This is the stuff of memories.'

Outside, the young officers of the law were preparing for the evening meal, cutting up fruit and onions. They'd taken their beds out of the tents to arrange a sleeping place on the grass for us. We had two beds, mosquito nets, two chairs, a table and an electric fan! Then a man from Rawalpindi arrived with two Five-Star supper boxes wrapped in blue cellophane and tied with yellow string and a green bow.

'Whow!' I exclaimed. 'This is more like it!'

I could barely contain my excitement in the face of such VIP treatment. All the aches and arguments of a hundred days, the irritations of the last few hours, simply evaporated. For me this was a 'wonderful place' for our last night on the move and the marvel of it was that we once believed we'd never get this far. Not even on the eightieth day so far into the trip, did we expect to reach the threshold of Rawalpindi. But it was more than that – at last we were on our way to acclaim.

'Only fourteen kilometres to go – not even fourteen miles!' exclaimed Ados. 'We can run that strongly.'

A few days before we wouldn't have contemplated running that far. Not all at once! But now the adrenalin was pumping and everything, we thought, seemed hunky-dory.

Richard: The last day started with my diary. I recorded a good sleep, a cool breeze, wake up time of five o'clock, a temperature of eighty-five degrees F and lots and lots of frogs on the ground last night.

I described breakfast as a 'blow out', too big and piggy to detail. I noted the arrival of 'droves of traffic police' to escort us into town. And the fact we had to delay leaving to time our finish for 10 am.

At ten past two that afternoon I picked up my diary again and noted, without an exclamation mark that 'It's all over.' I meant Part One. Part Two – the Press and TV side, the articles, slide shows, book and coming to terms with being celebrities – was just beginning.

A wonderful reception had been set up in Rawalpindi. The police shepherded us along our ten-mile route, television crews bobbed in and out of the trees, hung out of their vans. People lined the route as we neared the city and clapped. The police sounded their sirens and flashed their lights. We powered into the bazar, rounded a corner and saw a big red 'Himalayan Run' banner across the dual carriageway. We sprinted to the finish line and a cheering welcome at Flashman's Hotel.

A number of dignitaries were waiting for us: the British Ambassador, Sir Oliver Forster, and several Pakistani government officials – Mazood Nabi Nur from the Ministry of Culture; Major-General Qamar Ali Mirza of the Alpine Club of Pakistan; Mohsin Kamal, also Culture and Mr Munheeradin.

We were presented with a gold-tinted har, a ceremonial neck adornment, and some local kiddies garlanded us in roses and jasmines. Journalists bombarded us with questions, shoving microphones in front of us. Everyone tried grabbing us, pulling us this way and that.

'How do you feel?'

'What was it like?'

'Why did you do it?'

'Did you run all the way?'

What a marvellous fuss!

The rest of the day was equally demanding. We took phone calls galore, speaking to Dad and our sisters and a who's who of press, radio and television. *The Times*, the *Reading Post*, Radio Cumbria, Radio One, BBC Border TV, Australia Overnight Radio, the *Daily Express*, LBC, TV South, the Today Programme.

We gathered from home that we were in all the papers, and first item on the news. We had hit the publicity jackpot! General Zia al Haq, President of Pakistan, saw us on television and sent out the word 'Look after them'. As a result we were ensconced in the Islamabad Holiday Inn, courtesy of the Pakistani Government. We were very chuffed by this.

Back to bed, I made my final entry of Part I:

'We ran through a superb dust storm and then a torrential downpour this morning but by the time we got to Rawalpindi we had dried out. We timed our arrival at Flashman's to perfection, at 10.10, thanks to a half-hour rest, a half-hour BBC interview and a quarter-hour shit in the dust storm.'

Heaven knows, we could have got here sooner had I not had so many of those along the way.

Adrian: The running seemed so simple those last few hundred yards, as though someone else were doing the running for me. I never realised the end would come so suddenly, after so long, after 2000 miles, like a surprise. It had all been so endless. Now you cross a line and the adventure is over.

All over bar the cheering. And those important chaps saying 'congratulations, Mr Crane!' I'd never had to cope with being a hero before and I was a bit embarrassed: how could something so great be done by me! How pleased I was that I had tried!

128

Postscript

THE INTERMEDIATE TECHNOLOGY sponsorship effort went on to raise over £50,000 for their work all over the world. If you feel that 'Small is Beautiful' and that people should be helped to help themselves then join the race against poverty with Intermediate Technology.

One of us went off to marry Karen and had a baby boy, the other works for British Petroleum as an exploration geologist. Thanks partly to our high-altitude efforts in the Himalayas, we won Foster's Quadrathon non-stop in 16 hrs 26 mins 49 secs; 2 ml sea-swim, 50 kms race-walk, 100 ml bicycle, and full 26.2 ml marathon to finish.

On our Himalayan journey we each had; one set of thermal underwear, one cotton shirt, one pair of cotton trousers, one set of Gore-tex weatherwear, a pair of gloves, a balaclava, a pair of socks and a pair of shoes, a down duvet, a down sleeping bag, a picture of our girlfriends, a rucksack to put it all in and a plastic teaspoon to eat with. We shared camera, diaries, maps, passports, a list of songs and medical tips written on a piece of airmail paper, a handful of pills, a penknife, four safety pins, a plastic water jar and a lot of optimism.

We don't think we'll try that again.